50 MAKES
FOR MODERN
miniatures

DECORATE AND FURNISH
YOUR DIY DOLL HOUSE

50 MAKES FOR MODERN miniatures

DECORATE AND FURNISH YOUR DIY DOLL HOUSE

Chelsea Andersson

DAVID & CHARLES

www.davidandcharles.com

Contents

Introduction

I've never met someone who didn't like miniatures. There is something so inherently sweet – downright magical – about holding a teeny, tiny version of something you know so well.

I loved miniatures as a kid. I made dresses for my dolls out of socks, chairs out of recycled cardboard, and dinner plates from buttons. It was fun to look at ordinary objects and dream up ways to transform them into miniature creations. Because these creations didn't require much material, it was easy to make them from what I already had on hand. Digging through the recycling bin, there was always material to be repurposed. Every tiny scrap had potential.

This accessibility is what brought me back to miniatures as an adult. Fresh out of college and living in a tiny California apartment, I had neither the funds nor the space to design the home of my dreams. I wanted to create art and furniture – but each project required large amounts of materials and tools that I didn't have. By making furniture in miniature, I could explore hundreds of techniques and styles without running out of room or breaking the bank. It was limitless creativity in a tiny package.

Whether you're an experienced mini maker or just getting started, I encourage you to explore, get creative, and have fun. Use what you have on hand and take a peek at what you can recycle and repurpose. Introduce your own style to each of the projects in this book.

As you work through the makes, look for ways to customize and expand them. Bring your own style, color, and experience to each design. Apply what you learn here to the creation of any tiny object. After all, these projects are merely the beginning of your great miniature adventure.

Tools & Materials

Before you get started, take some time to familiarize yourself with the tools and materials you'll be using. Take a look around your home to see what you already have on hand and work from there.

Workspace Prep

Even miniature projects can make a big mess, so it's best to keep supplies on hand to tidy up as you work. For spills, paper towels are a must. Alcohol wipes and rubbing alcohol are great tools for cleaning up excess glue or paint as well as just keeping your hands clean. Scrap cardboard and paper cups are ideal for mixing paint and they're easy to dispose of afterward.

Tools

When first starting out, use what tools you have on hand. This might include office supplies, found objects, or even full-size power tools. For a more refined approach, the tools shown here will allow you to work with greater detail and accuracy.

Cutting mat
A self-healing cutting mat protects your work surface, allows you to make cuts more easily, and often has grid markers to help with quick measuring.

Craft knife and spare blades (1)
Craft knives with replaceable blades allow you to make intricate cuts in paper and wood. The fine point is ideal for exact cuts and narrow radii. Maintaining a sharp blade will ensure your cuts are accurate and clean. Always change the blade at the first sign of wear.

Jeweler's saw and spare blades (2)
A jeweler's saw typically has a replaceable blade, two tightening points, and a handle. Blades with varying teeth will allow you to cut through a wide variety of materials such as metal and wood with ease. The key is to work slowly to maintain control of the cut.

Miniature miter saw and box (3)
A miter saw and box are great for cutting wood or metal dowels. The miter box typically has a 90-degree cut line as well as a 45-degree line.

Scissors – fabric and other (4)
A sharp pair of scissors will allow you to make controlled detail cuts in a variety of materials, including paper, cardboard, and fibers.

Wire cutters and pliers (5)
Wire cutters will help you snip through the small metal wires, rods, and paper clips needed for creating the plants, hangers, and any other wire-based project those might inspire. Pliers will allow you to bend that wire into a variety of shapes.

Glues (6)
There are several kinds of glue that you will find useful when making miniatures.

- PVA or craft glue is great for fast attachments. It dries clear with some flexibility. You can also use watered-down craft glue as a kind of varnish on paper-based projects.

- Wood glue: Use wood glue whenever you are attaching wood to wood. It's very durable and can be sanded and painted.

- Cyanoacrylate glue (super glue) is acrylic resin based and forms a tight bond where any moisture is present. It's a good alternative if you run into any issues with other glues not holding.

- Hot glue is not the most durable adhesive, but it's a great option for quick or temporary attachments.

Metal ruler with cork backing (7)

Any ruler will work for measurements, but as a cutting aid, you'll want to use a metal ruler. A plastic or wooden ruler can be scratched or damaged by the craft knife and become unusable. The cork backing keeps the ruler from sliding on your material.

Metal square

A metal square can be used to make perfect 90- or 45-degree cuts.

Sanding sponges and sandpaper (8)

Sanding sponges are flexible blocks wrapped with sandpaper. The flexible surface is easy to hold and manipulate around the material. Traditional sandpaper can also be used.

Battery-powered rotary sander (9)

For more advanced makers, a rotary sander is great for quick sanding. They typically come with a variety of attachments that you may find useful for cutting, sanding, or drilling.

Pin vise (10)

A pin vise is a hand-powered drill. It allows for delicate control.

Binder clips (11)

Binder clips act as miniature clamps. They provide a strong connection when creasing material or waiting for connections to dry.

Masking tape (12)

Masking tape can be used to hold materials together as they dry. It also acts as a flexible connection in lieu of miniature hinges. Electrical tape, which is slightly more dense and tacky than masking tape, can be used for hinges where addiAonal strength and durability is needed.

Embroidery hoop and needle (13)

A small embroidery hoop allows you to hold fabric taut while painting, drawing, or embroidering it. Use a standard sewing needle for upholstery projects, and a larger embroidery needle for decorative embellishments.

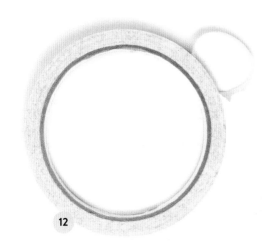

⅛in (3mm) basswood sheet

⅛in (3mm) round wooden dowels

⅛in (3mm) square wooden dowels

¼in (6mm) square wooden dowels

¼ x ⅛in (6 x 3mm) rectangular wooden dowels

Wood Materials

Wood is a versatile material for miniatures. It can be easily cut, shaped, sanded, painted, or stained.

Basswood (1)

Basswood or balsa sheets are perfect for larger areas of miniatures, such as table tops, as they are soft and relatively easy to cut by hand. Solid wood sheets are easier to cut through than plywood, which has dense layers of glue. Basswood is slightly more dense and will allow the completed miniatures to be a bit more durable. For the projects in this book, use a wood thickness of approximately ⅛in (3mm). These wood sheets can be cut using a combination of a craft knife and a jeweler's saw.

Wooden dowels (2)

Wooden dowels come in a variety of lengths and thicknesses and are a great way to add design detail to your pieces. Larger square and rectangular dowels can be used to make miniature furniture. Round dowels can be used to create hinged furnishings with parts that move.

Coffee stirrers (3)

Coffee stirrers are affordable and multi purpose. As a tool they can be used to mix paint or apply glue. As a material, they work well for floor boards, framing, or wherever thin pieces of wood are needed.

Toothpicks (4)

Toothpicks have an even taper at both ends, which makes them the perfect match for spindle furniture. They can also be used to clear excess glue and paint tiny details.

Wooden beads (5)

Wooden beads can be used as miniature planter pots, a lamp base, and as a tool for forming clay. Small wooden beads can be stacked to create ornate candle holders.

Fabric & Fiber

Creating a convincing miniature with fabric can be difficult. Unlike wood which can be sanded down, or metal which comes in a wide range of gauges and sizes, fabric maintains its thickness whether you are making a full-size or a miniature project. As a result, seams can often appear overstuffed or out of scale. In most cases, only a small amount of fabric is needed. The perfect piece of fabric might already be waiting for you in your scrap bin or rag pile. Many stores sell off-cuts or fabric ends at a discount.

Cotton fabric (1)
It is easiest to use fabric materials that are naturally thinner for miniature projects. Cotton fabric used for quilting is perfect for miniature upholstering.

Woven fabrics (2)
Slightly heavier woven fabrics such as aida cloth, monk's cloth, and bulkier decorative pieces are ideal for rugs and blankets. Aida cloth and monk's cloth are even-weave fabrics and can be easily embroidered and decorated. Decorative woven fabrics need only a little finessing to become believable scale rugs.

Faux leather (3)
Faux leather and "waxed" faux-leather paper are great alternatives to thick leather. For stiffer fabrics, a thin cotton canvas fabric is ideal. Explore different patterns and colors as a way of bringing a unique finish to your miniature pieces.

Embroidery floss (4)
Colorful embroidery floss and string are perfect substitutes where rope or yarn might be used at full scale. You will also need thread for hand sewing soft-furnishing elements. Twine can be used in lieu of jute, or wicker. For quilts, cushions, and bedding, you will need a fabric filler such as cotton batting or toy filler. Consider using stuffing from an old pillow or fabric scraps as a filler.

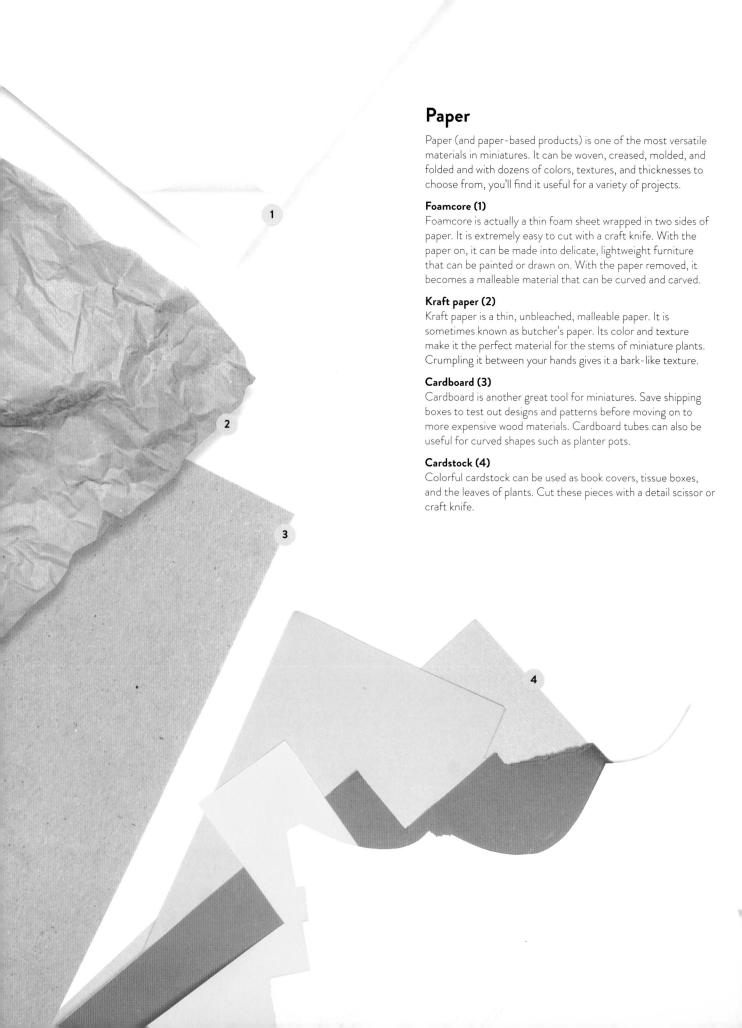

Paper

Paper (and paper-based products) is one of the most versatile materials in miniatures. It can be woven, creased, molded, and folded and with dozens of colors, textures, and thicknesses to choose from, you'll find it useful for a variety of projects.

Foamcore (1)

Foamcore is actually a thin foam sheet wrapped in two sides of paper. It is extremely easy to cut with a craft knife. With the paper on, it can be made into delicate, lightweight furniture that can be painted or drawn on. With the paper removed, it becomes a malleable material that can be curved and carved.

Kraft paper (2)

Kraft paper is a thin, unbleached, malleable paper. It is sometimes known as butcher's paper. Its color and texture make it the perfect material for the stems of miniature plants. Crumpling it between your hands gives it a bark-like texture.

Cardboard (3)

Cardboard is another great tool for miniatures. Save shipping boxes to test out designs and patterns before moving on to more expensive wood materials. Cardboard tubes can also be useful for curved shapes such as planter pots.

Cardstock (4)

Colorful cardstock can be used as book covers, tissue boxes, and the leaves of plants. Cut these pieces with a detail scissor or craft knife.

Everything Else

There are dozens of everyday items that can be used as scale objects or mini tools. For example, bottle caps can be used as planters and buttons and washers can be used as formers when shaping things from polymer clay. Push your creativity by using what you already have.

Throughout this book, a number of additional materials will be used to bring your miniature creations to life. These are some of the most useful.

Wire (1)
Wire in various thicknesses can be formed into hangers, plant stems, and sink faucets. Use wire cutters to trim as needed and needle-nose pliers to bend and shape it.

Paint (2)
Spray paint is recommended whenever a project will be completely colored, as it allows for a smooth, even finish. For small details, or where control is needed, acrylic paint is best. For wood projects, oil or water based stains can be applied to enhance the texture. A stain-like appearance can also be achieved by using watered down brown paint.

Polymer clay (3)
Polymer clay is a malleable craft material that hardens when baked. It is available in dozens of colors, but can also be painted once cured. It can be shaped using everyday items like wooden beads, dowels, and metal washers, or speciality tools like metal clay cutters.

Additives and fillers (4)
Baking soda can be added to paint to create a gritty, concrete-like texture. Heat-set fabric painting medium is a paint additive that allows paint to be applied to fabric more evenly and permanently. Fine surface filler and wood filler can be used to refine your projects. Use wood filler to fill gaps when assembling wood furnishings. Fine surface filler can be used to create a textured or smooth surface like faux porcelain. Cornstarch should be used as needed to reduce tackiness in polymer clay.

Mirrored vinyl (5)
Mirrored vinyl is used to create DIY-friendly mirrors. It has an adhesive backing and can be cut with just a pair of scissors.

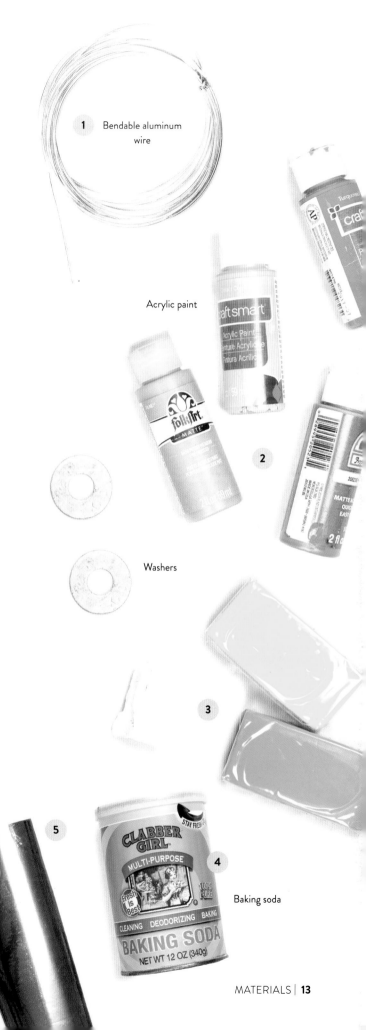

1 Bendable aluminum wire

Acrylic paint

Washers

Bendable craft wire

Baking soda

Techniques

Throughout this book you will find several recurring techniques. Refer back to these pages whenever you need a more detailed description of assembly, cutting, painting, and more.

Scale

Staying consistent with one scale will ensure that all of the elements in your project work well together and look believable. The most common scale for dollhouses is 1:12. If you use the imperial system, 1:12 always works out to being the easiest scale to calculate, because 1in = 1ft. For example, if you had a 12 x 12in (30 x 30cm) box that you wanted to recreate in 12-scale, it would be 1 x 1in. The projects in this book are designed for 12-scale.

Painting

Painting can completely transform a miniature creation. The techniques below can add texture, dimension, and detail to a variety of materials.

1. Dry brushing: This is a technique that allows for a rough or imperfect textured appearance. To achieve this look, dip just the very tip of a dry paint brush into acrylic paint. Gently dab or sweep the dry brush across your surface to create the slightest amount of color variance.

2. Watered-down paint: Mixing a small amount of water with acrylic paint enables you to create a slightly translucent coating. This is a great way to add detail to paper plants, wood finishes, or even to create a distressed/weathered look.

3. Faux concrete paint: Mix 3 parts baking soda with 2 parts acrylic paint to create a texture that is similar to concrete. Apply to surfaces with a coffee stirrer, paint brush, or even your fingertips. If mixed with red/orange paints, this same technique can be used to represent terracotta.

Tip: *The goal is to create a slightly gritty paint – a texture that feels sandy, but can still be easily spread across a surface. Add more paint or baking soda to create this texture as needed.*

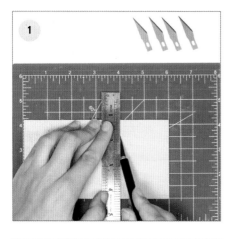

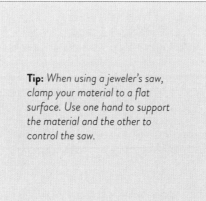

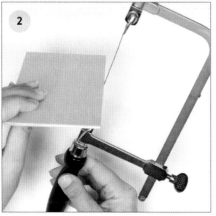

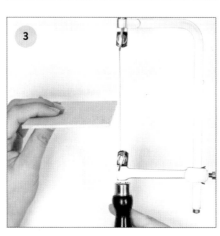

Tip: *When using a jeweler's saw, clamp your material to a flat surface. Use one hand to support the material and the other to control the saw.*

Cutting

There are four main techniques for cutting project materials. For paper and fibers, scissors will work just fine. For wood materials, use a craft knife, a jeweler's saw, or a miter saw. Many of these tools can be used interchangeably. Test out each technique and work with whatever feels most comfortable for you.

1. Metal ruler and craft knife: When cutting straight lines in wood or paper, consider using a metal ruler and a craft knife with a fresh blade. Align your ruler to the edge of your template or design, and cut on the outside edge of the material. Replace the craft knife blade frequently to ensure a smooth cut without damage to the project or yourself.

2–3. Jeweler's saw: A jeweler's saw is most commonly used for curves in wood or metal. Its extremely fine blade allows you to manipulate it into sharp corners of mini projects.

4. Miter saw and box: For perpendicular cuts along dowels, a miter saw is ideal. The miter box holds your material in place while the sharp teeth of the saw work their way through thick material.

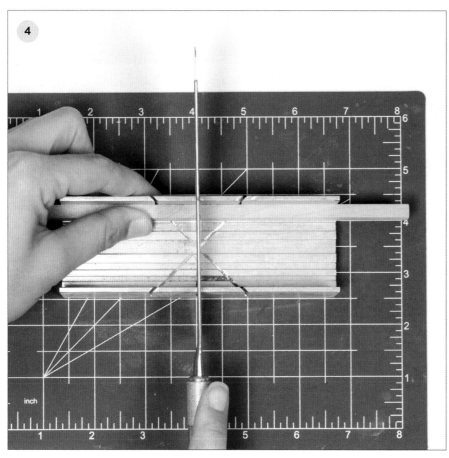

Sanding

After cutting wood materials, it may be helpful to finely sand the edges before assembly. Lower grit sandpaper removes more material to create rounded edges. Higher grit sandpapers are great for refining wood pieces to an even finish.

Finishing Wood

Stains and basic mineral oils can be used to finish the piece and accentuate the natural tone and grain of the wood. Wood stains should be applied before your furniture is assembled. Any excess glue coverage will resist stain and leave an inconsistent coating.

If you are painting your wood pieces, apply thin layers of acrylic or spray paint and seal with a clear protective coating.

Polymer Clay

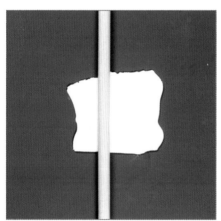
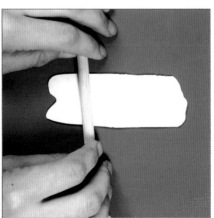

Polymer clay is a malleable craft material that hardens when baked. Baking times and temperatures vary by manufacturer, so review the material packaging for details.

Always work with clean hands on a dust-free surface, as polymer clay easily picks up smudges and dirt.

All polymer clay needs to be "conditioned" before it can be molded. To do this, work the polymer clay between your hands or with a small rolling pin to soften the material.

Tip: *There is a fine line between conditioned and over-conditioned polymer clay. If you find that your clay is too sticky or won't separate from your work surface, place it in a fridge or freezer for a few minutes to firm back up.*

Assembly

Many projects in this book require precise alignment. To ensure that your pieces are perpendicular, it is helpful to work directly on a cutting mat that has measurement markers.

Ensure that pieces are properly supported when assembling. Use binder clips or masking tape to hold delicate pieces in place.

If you see gaps after assembly, fill them with wood filler or fine surface filler. This will enable you to achieve a smooth finished product.

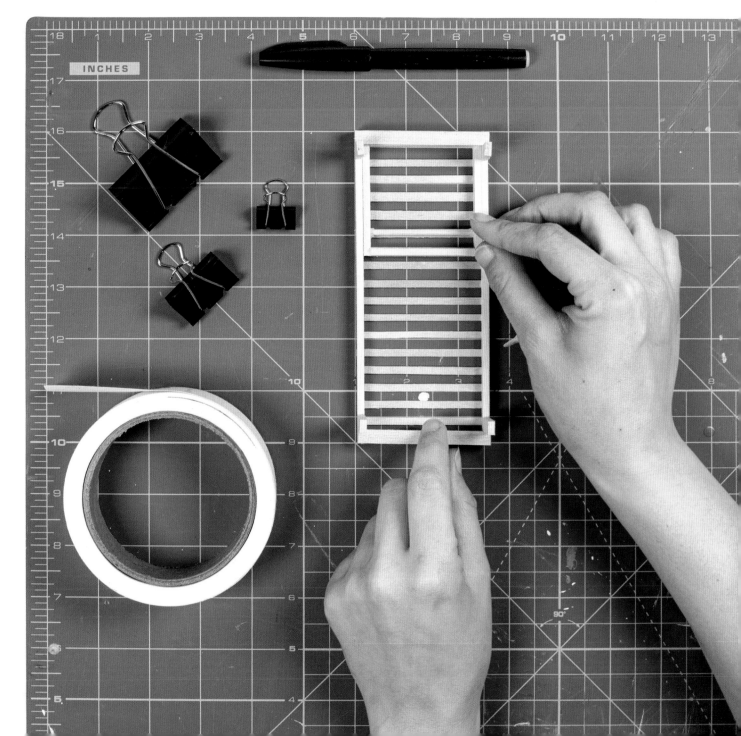

LIVING ROOM

Sofa

A sofa is going to be one of the coziest spots in your dollhouse and will be the focus of your living room. Choose a fabric whose color will blend with all of the other features of the living room. This no-sew approach to mini upholstery makes this DIY an easy introduction.

Materials

- ¼in (6mm) square wooden dowels
- ⅛in (3mm) basswood sheet
- Wood glue
- Craft glue
- Foamcore
- Cotton batting
- Cotton canvas fabric
- Masking tape

Tools

- Miter saw and box
- Metal ruler
- Craft knife and cutting mat
- Fabric scissors

MAKE THE SOFA

Refer to Templates: Sofa Structure for details of what to cut.

1 Cut the ¼in (6mm) square wooden dowel pieces (A–D) using a miter saw and box. Cut the rectangular sofa base (E) from a ⅛in (3mm) basswood sheet, using a craft knife on a cutting mat.

2 To make the side pieces/armrests, place one A and one C piece upright, using a ruler to check that they are parallel to each other. Apply wood glue to attach a B piece between them, aligning it with the top edge of piece A. Repeat to create the second armrest.

3 Glue two D pieces and two B pieces together to form a rectangle, as shown.

4 Glue piece E to the top to complete the sofa base.

5 Apply glue to a D piece and use it to connect the tops of the two side pieces.

6 Apply glue to the remaining D piece and align it with the tops of the armrests.

7 Glue the seat assembly to the armrests, approximately ½in (1.2cm) from the bottom of the sofa.

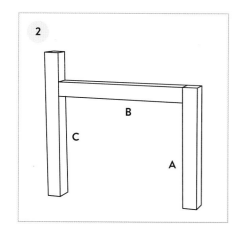

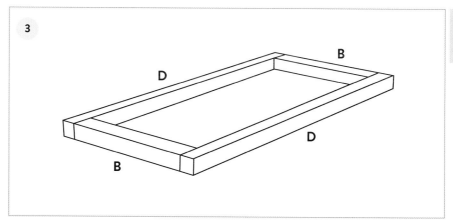

Tip: *This project requires many precise measurements and 90-degree connections. It may be helpful to assemble all the elements on a cutting mat marked with a grid.*

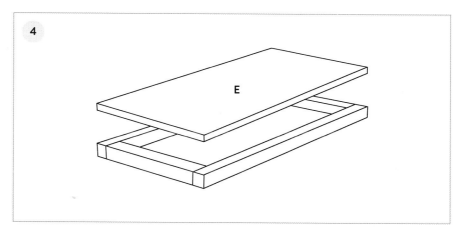

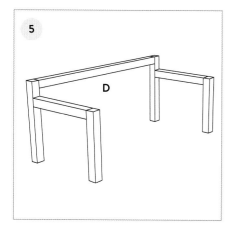

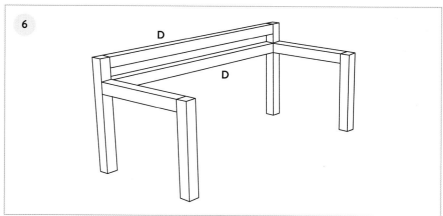

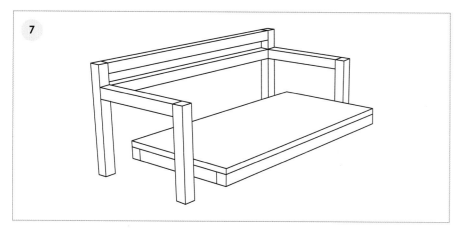

Tip: *Use masking tape to hold pieces together as they dry.*

Tip: *Iron fabric before you cut it to ensure accurate measurements.*

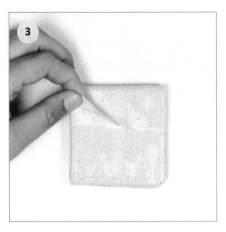

Tip: *Test fit the fabic to the cushion forms before applying glue to be sure that it all fits properly.*

MAKE THE CUSHIONS

Refer to Templates: Sofa Cushions for details of what to cut.

1 Cut the foamcore using a craft knife and metal ruler. Cut the batting and fabric using scissors. Using craft glue, stick two pieces of foamcore and one piece of cotton batting together to create the cushion form. Repeat to make a second cushion form.

2 Place the cushion form on the cotton canvas fabric, batting side down. Fold the rectangular sides up over the base. Align the thin tabs with the edge of the cushion to cover the corners. Glue in place.

3 Fold the remaining sides up over the cushion and glue in place. Flip over to reveal the completed cushion. Repeat steps 2 and 3 to make the second cushion.

4 Cut two 4 x 4in (10 x 10cm) pieces of fabric for the backrest cushion covers. Center the backrest foamcore pieces on the fabric. Cut notches into the fabric to form around the backrest. Fold the fabric over the foamcore and glue in place.

Rug

Rugs are a great way to introduce color and pattern to a room. This simple tutorial will allow you to make dozens of unique rugs quickly. Source a variety of woven fabric scraps and use this method to create rugs of varying dimensions.

Materials
- Woven fabric
- Craft glue

Tools
- Fabric scissors
- Pencil
- Ruler
- Ttoothpick

MAKE THE RUG

1 Use fabric scissors to cut a 4¼ x 6¼in (11 x 16cm) rectangle from a woven fabric. On the wrong (non-printed) side of the fabric, draw a pencil line all around, ¼in (6mm) from the edge.

2 Using a toothpick, loosen the horizontal fibers between the pencil line and the fabric edge.

3 Gently fray the edges of the fabric by removing one strand of thread at a time.

4 To prevent your fabric from fraying further, apply a small amount of craft glue to the underside of the rug.

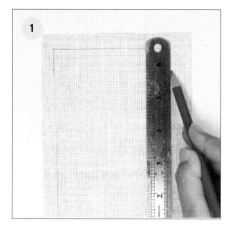

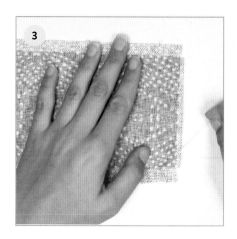

Bookshelf & Books

This ladder-style bookshelf is the perfect place to showcase dozens of miniature creations. Adorn it with books, plants, and other mini accessories that you make or purchase along the way. Customize your books with decorative covers and by varying sizes and numbers of pages.

Materials

- ¼in (6mm) square wooden dowels
- ⅛in (3mm) basswood sheet
- Wood glue
- Masking tape
- White and colored cardstock
- Craft glue

Tools

- Miter saw and box
- Craft knife and cutting mat
- Metal ruler
- Pencil

MAKE THE BOOKSHELF

Refer to Templates: Bookshelf for details of what to cut.

1 Cut the ¼in (6mm) square wooden dowel pieces (A–C) using a miter saw and box. Cut the rectangular shelves (D–G) from a ⅛in (3mm) basswood sheet, using a craft knife on a cutting mat.

2 Glue parts A, B, and C together to form a triangle. The opening should be approximately 2in (5cm) wide. Repeat to create the second side of the shelf.

Tip: *Assemble pieces on a cutting mat with a grid to ensure that the widest part of the bookshelf opening is 2in (5cm).*

---

3 Align the two sides together along the A piece. Starting at the bottom, use a pencil to mark 1in (2.5cm) intervals across the material. This is where you will attach the shelves.

4 Add a small amount of wood glue to the pencil marks and attach the shelves in order from smallest to largest. Use masking tape as needed to support the structure while it dries.

5 Allow to dry completely before adding decoration and accessories.

MAKE THE BOOKS

1 Using your metal ruler and craft knife, cut eight 1 x ¾in (2.5 x 2cm) rectangles from white cardstock.

2 Stack the "pages" and align them along one side.

3 Cut a 1 x 1⅝in (2.5 x 4.2cm) strip of colored cardstock to create the book cover and score a straight line ¾in (2cm) from each edge; this creates the "spine" of the book.

4 Apply craft glue to the edge of the pages.

5 Fold the cover over the binding and press to fix it in place.

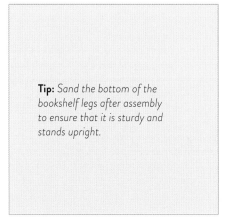

Tip: *Sand the bottom of the bookshelf legs after assembly to ensure that it is sturdy and stands upright.*

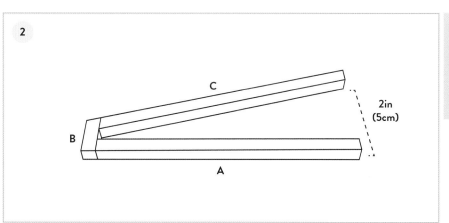

2in
(5cm)

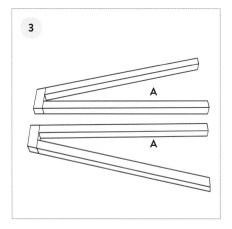

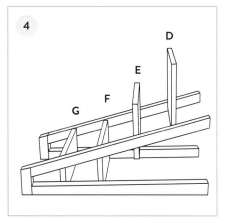

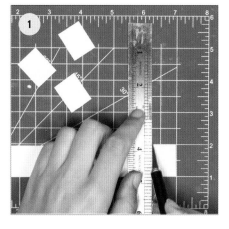

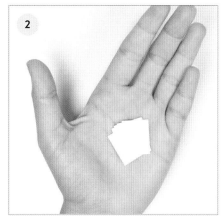

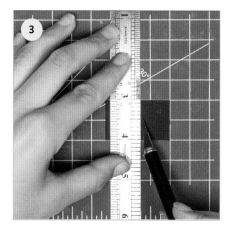

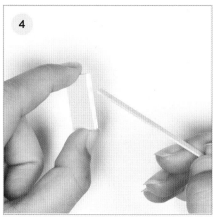

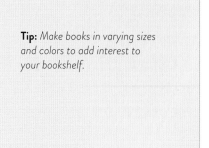

Tip: *Make books in varying sizes and colors to add interest to your bookshelf.*

Plant & Pot

Planter pots are a great way to use recycled materials in miniatures. Search through your recycling bin for plastic bottle caps of various sizes. For this project, a small bottle cap (from a tube of toothpaste or a sauce bottle, for example) will work best. The concrete texture is created using a combination of acrylic paint and baking soda.

Materials

- Recycled bottle cap
- Medium gray, dark gray, dark green, and lime green acrylic paints
- Baking soda
- Light green cardstock
- Craft glue

Tools

- Sanding sponge
- Scrap cardboard or paper cup for mixing materials
- Coffee stirrer (optional)
- Fine paint brush
- Craft knife and cutting mat
- Detail scissors
- Round wooden dowel

MAKE THE POT

1   Using a sanding sponge, gently brush all sides of the recycled bottle cap. This will create a rough surface for the faux concrete mixture to adhere to.

2   Mix the faux concrete paint from baking soda and medium gray acrylic paint (see Techniques: Painting). Apply the mixture to all sides of the bottle cap, using a coffee stirrer or your fingers. Be sure to cover the bottom and inner rim of the planter.

3   Once dry, "dry brush" (see Techniques: Painting) a small amount of dark gray acrylic paint onto the faux concrete surface.

MAKE THE PLANT

1   Use a craft knife to cut a 4 x 4in (10 x 10cm) piece of light green cardstock. Use a fine paint brush and lightly watered-down dark green paint to paint thin stripes in one direction. Keep your lines narrow and close together—no more than ⅛in (3mm) apart. Allow the paper to dry, then repeat the process on the opposite side.

2   Using your detail scissors or a craft knife, cut approximately 20 tapered leaves 1–2½in (2.5–6.5cm) in length. Each leaf should be approximately ¼in (6mm) wide at the base.

3   Using lime green paint, gently outline each leaf with a tiny stroke of color and let dry.

4   Apply a coat of watered-down craft glue to both sides of each leaf and let dry.

5   Use a wooden dowel to gently shape each leaf; begin by curling the leaf vertically around the dowel.

6   Add variation to the leaves by gently wrapping them around the dowel horizontally.

7   Glue your completed leaves into the concrete planter using craft glue.

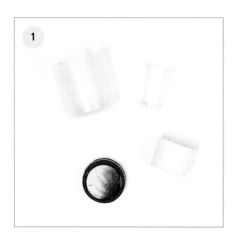

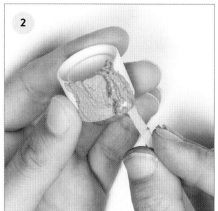

Tip: *Use a small amount of paint at a time so as to not oversaturate the paper. Imperfection is great; it makes the plant more realistic!*

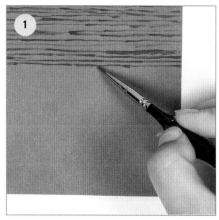

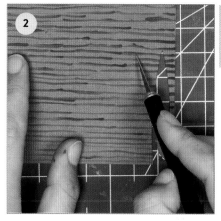

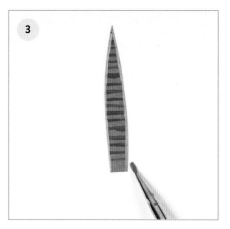

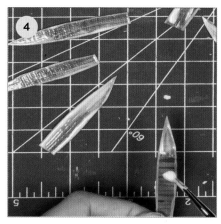

Tip: *When shaping the leaves, just a tiny bit of pressure will do!*

Lounge Chair

This modern lounge chair makes use of waxed faux-leather paper to give the illusion of fine upholstery. This fabric-like paper is flexible while still maintaining its shape and durability. The chair's structure is made of durable 1/4in (6mm) rectangular dowels. Finish the wood with your preferred paint or stain to fully customize the design.

Materials

- ¼in (6mm) square wooden dowels
- Waxed faux-leather paper or cotton fabric
- Paint or wood stain (optional)
- Wood glue
- Craft glue

Tools

- Miter saw and box or craft knife and cutting mat
- Fabric scissors
- Paint brush (optional)
- Masking tape or binder clips

MAKE THE CHAIR

Refer to Templates: Lounge Chair for details of what to cut.

1 Cut the chair pieces (A–F) from ¼in (6mm) square wooden dowel, using a miter saw and box or a craft knife on a cutting mat.

2 Cut the fabric back and seat pieces (G and H) from waxed faux-leather paper (or your fabric of choice), using a craft knife or fabric scissors.

3 Use wood glue to connect parts A, B, and C, as shown. Repeat for the second side.

4 Use wood glue to connect parts D and E, as shown. Allow to dry. Repeat for the second side.

5 Attach the arms to either side of the chair back assemblies ½in (1.2cm) from the front edge of part C. Use masking tape as a clamp to hold things in place if needed.

6 Be sure that the arms are glued to the outside edges of the chair back assembly.

7 Use wood glue to attach the remaining part E as a brace between the two front legs, positioning it ½in (1.2cm) up from the bottom of the legs. Attach part F between the two back legs, ¼in (6mm) up from the bottom of the legs. Use masking tape or binder clips to hold everything in place and allow the chair to dry completely before attaching the fabric back and seat.

8 Apply craft glue to the four tabs of part G, the chair back. Wrap the tabs around the chair back to secure and use masking tape to ensure that it dries in the correct position.

9 Repeat this process with part H, the chair seat.

Tip: Use a cutting mat with grid markings to ensure that your pieces are perfectly "square."

3

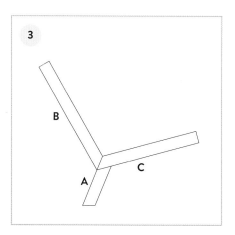

4

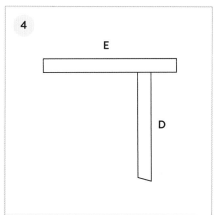

5

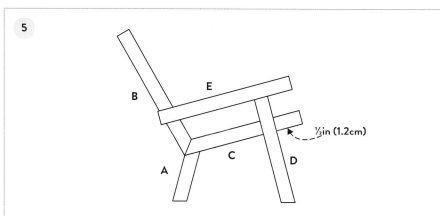

6

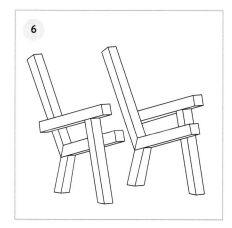

7

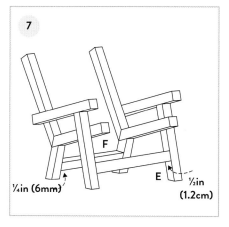

8

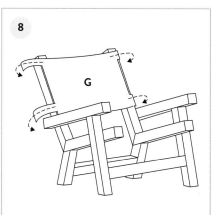

9

Coffee Table

Combined with tapered legs, this organic-shaped coffee table will give a mid-century feel to an otherwise modern room. Customize the table by changing up the shape of the top, adding a splash of color with paint, or staining the wood for a natural look. Decorate your mini table with books, a mug, or other tiny accessories.

Materials
- ⅛in (3mm) basswood sheet
- Wood glue

Tools
- Craft knife and cutting mat or jeweler's saw
- Sanding sponge (optional)

MAKE THE COFFEE TABLE

Refer to Templates: Coffee Table for details of what to cut.

1 Cut the table top and legs from a ⅛in (3mm) basswood sheet, using a craft knife on a cutting mat or a jeweler's saw.

2 Place the table top on a flat surface.

3 Apply a small amount of wood glue to the end of each leg. Place two legs at the wider end of the table and one at the narrow end, making sure that they taper outward – away from the center of the table.

4 Allow the table to dry fully before turning it right side up.

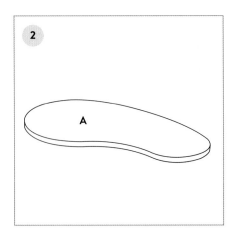

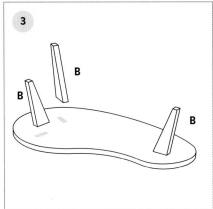

Tip: *Round the edges of each piece with a sanding sponge, to give a softer look.*

Wall Art

With miniature wall art, you can create custom artwork in seconds. Clip images from your favorite magazine, buy digital downloads from artists on Etsy, or even draw or paint your own! There are so many great ways to make mini art. For this piece of wall art, we will create an abstract image that is sure to match the rest of your living room.

Materials

- White cardstock
- Wood coffee stirrer
- Acrylic paint (any color)
- Craft glue
- White embroidery floss

Tools

- Craft knife and cutting mat
- Paint brush
- Permanent marker or paint pen

MAKE THE WALL ART

1 Cut a 2 x 3in (5 x 7.5cm) rectangle of white cardstock and two 2in (5cm) strips of wood coffee stirrer.

2 Select a color and give your cardstock a single rough coat of paint. Allow to dry.

3 With a black permanent marker or paint pen, doodle a small flower. Again, imperfection is great! Your flower can have sharp edges, go off the page, etc!

Tip: *This artwork will look great if your background paint is somewhat imperfect – streaky, patchy, and unused white space are all good!*

4 Using craft glue, stick one strip of coffee stirrer to the top of the artwork and the other to the bottom.

5 Cut a 3in (7.5cm) length of embroidery floss and attach the ends to the back of the artwork. Hang your artwork from the floss with a small piece of tape.

Lamp

This mid-century-inspired lamp mixes multiple materials for a realistic look. Customize it by using patterned or colored fabric for the lampshade. To make this light functional, consider purchasing a mini battery-powered LED.

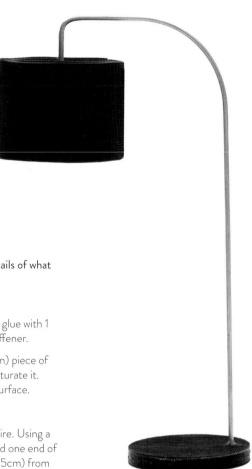

Materials

- Craft glue
- Cyanoacrylate glue (super glue)
- Water
- Cotton fabric of choice
- Approx. 10in (25cm) of 8-gauge (3.2mm) bendable aluminum wire
- Acrylic paint (optional)
- ⅛in (3mm) basswood sheet
- 4 toothpicks
- Small wooden bead

Tools

- Paper cup
- Coffee stirrer
- Fabric scissors
- Wire cutters
- Needle-nose pliers
- Craft knife and cutting mat or jeweler's saw
- Pin vise and ⅛in (3mm) drill bit
- Paint brush (optional)
- Masking tape

MAKE THE LAMP

Refer to Templates: Lamp for details of what to cut.

Prepare the lampshade fabric

1   In a paper cup, mix 1 part craft glue with 1 part water to act as a fabric stiffener.

2   Submerge a 3 x 7in (7.5 x 18cm) piece of cotton fabric in the cup and saturate it. Dry flat on a water-resistant surface.

Form the lamp

3   Cut a 10in (25cm) length of wire. Using a pair of needle-nose pliers, bend one end of the wire at a right angle, 1in (2.5cm) from the end.

4   Find a hard, round object in your home that is 2in (5cm) in diameter or larger.

Tip: *This is how we will form the arch in our lamp. Try a vase, a tin can, or a cup.*

---

5   Bend the top of the wire around the object to create a quarter circle near the right angle.

Build the lamp

6   Use a craft knife and/or jeweler's saw to cut the lamp pieces from a ⅛in (3mm) basswood sheet. Using a pin vise, drill ⅛in (3mm) holes in parts A, C, and D where indicated on the templates.

7   Cut four toothpicks to 1½in (4cm) in length. Insert them into pieces C and D where indicated on the templates to create a cylinder.

8   Paint if desired and allow to dry.

9   Cut your dry stiff cotton fabric into a 1½ x 6½in (4 x 16.5cm) strip. Apply a thin line of craft glue along both long edges of the fabric, then wrap it around the edges of the lampshade. Allow to dry, temporarily securing with masking tape if required.

Assemble the lamp

10   Insert the wire into the hole in part A and use cyanoacrylate glue (super glue) to secure.

11   When dry, use super glue to attach the lampshade to the small bend at the end of the wire. Add a small wooden bead to anchor the lampshade and act as a "light bulb."

3–5

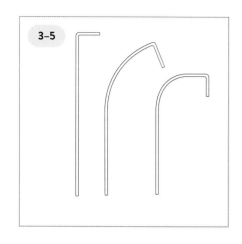

6

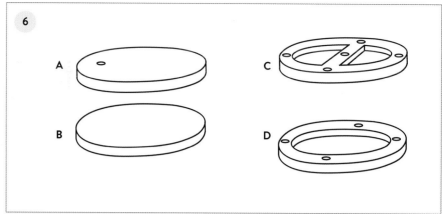

A

B

C

D

7

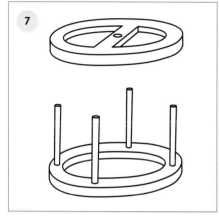

8

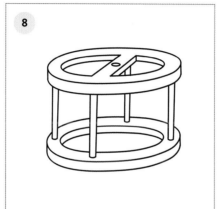

9

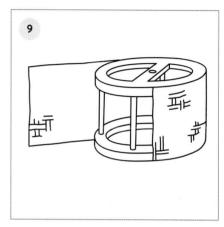

10

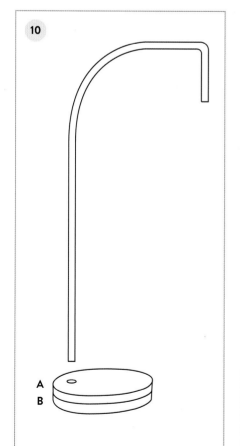

A
B

11

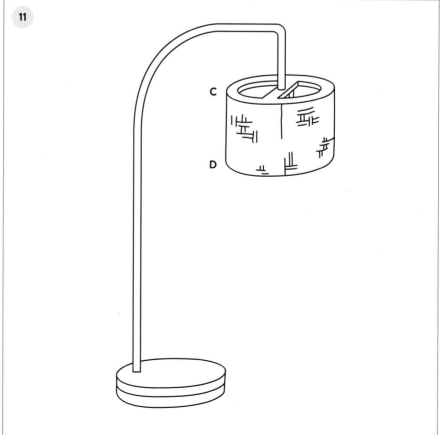

C

D

DINING ROOM

Dining Chair

This miniature spindle chair is a modern take on a classic dining chair. It looks great in either natural wood or painted in a bright color. Make four or more chairs to create a complete dining set.

Materials

- ⅛in (3mm) basswood sheet
- 4 toothpicks
- Wood glue
- Paint or wood stain (optional)
- Masking tape

Tools

- Jeweler's saw or craft knife and cutting mat
- Pin vise and ¹⁄₁₆in (1.5mm) drill bit
- Sanding sponge
- Paint brush (optional)

MAKE THE DINING CHAIR

Refer to Templates: Dining Chair for details of what to cut.

1 Use a jeweler's saw or a craft knife on a cutting mat to cut the pieces from a ⅛in (3mm) basswood sheet. Use a pin vise to drill ¹⁄₁₆in (1.5mm) holes in pieces A and C where indicated. Cut two toothpicks to 2in (5cm) in length and two toothpicks to 2¹⁄₁₆in (5.2cm) in length. Sand all components to give them a slightly rounded edge.

2 Glue parts B and C together.

3 Apply a small amount of wood glue to the drilled holes in part C. Insert the two smaller toothpicks into the center holes and the two longer toothpicks into the outside holes. Allow to dry.

4 Apply a small amount of wood glue to the unattached end of each toothpick and insert them into the drilled holes in part A. Use masking tape as needed to hold the backrest in place until dry.

5 Apply wood glue to the wide end of each leg and attach it to the underside of part A, positioning the legs evenly at the corners and ensuring that they taper away from the chair seat.

6 Optional: Paint if desired.

2

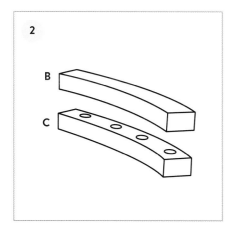

Tip: *Once the glue has fully dried, turn the chair upside down and gently sand the legs to ensure that it sits flat.*

3

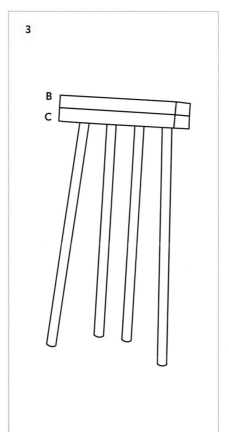

4

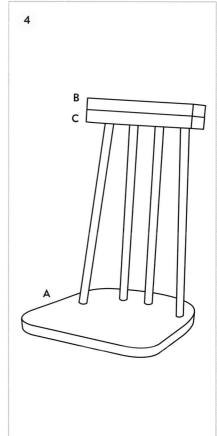

5

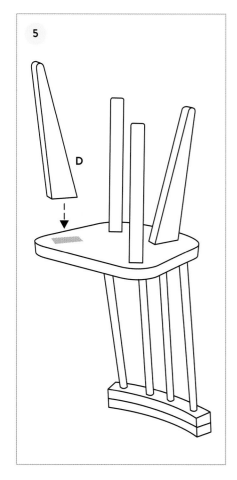

Dining Table

A simple table can make a miniature dining room feel warm and welcoming. The instructions here are for a rectangular dining table, but much of the process would be the same for a square, round, or oblong table top. Customize the dimensions and shape to best fit your miniature scene.

Materials
- ⅛in (3mm) basswood sheet
- Wood glue
- Paint or wood stain (optional)

Tools
- Jeweler's saw or craft knife and cutting mat
- Sanding sponge
- Pencil
- Ruler
- Paint brush (optional)

MAKE THE TABLE

Refer to Templates: Dining Table for details of what to cut.

1 Use a jeweler's saw or craft knife on a cutting mat to cut the pieces from a ⅛in (3mm) basswood sheet. Sand all components to give them a slightly rounded edge.

2 Use a ruler and pencil to mark a guideline ½in (1.2cm) in from the edge of the table top. This will allow you to position the legs accurately.

3 Apply a small amount of wood glue to the wide end of each table leg and attach them to the table top at the pencil markings, ensuring that they taper away from the table top.

4 Allow to dry fully.

5 Optional: Apply paint or wood stain to the table if desired.

1

A

Tip: *Round the edges of each piece with a sanding sponge for a softer appearance.*

Tip: *Support the table legs as they dry to ensure that they remain upright.*

2

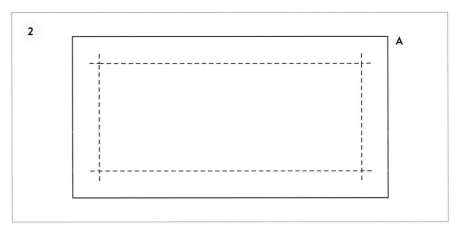

A

3

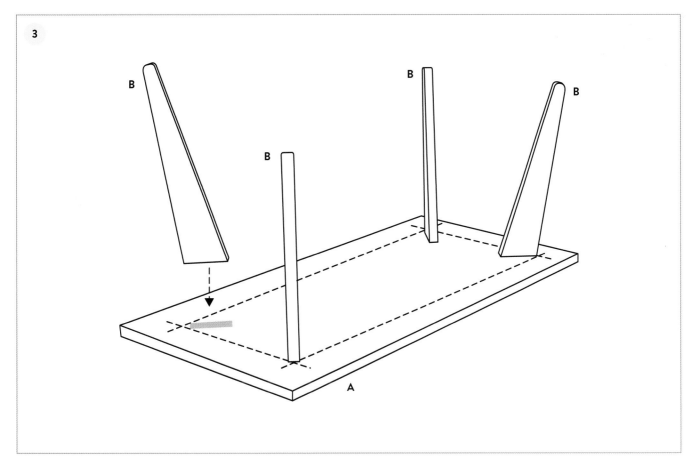

B   B   B

B

A

Fluted Planter

This planter is covered in wooden dowels to create a textured finish. A larger diameter will allow it to be used for a small indoor tree. Modify these instructions to make smaller-diameter table-top planters.

Materials

- Paper or cardboard tube, 1–1½in (2.5–4cm) in diameter
- Cardboard
- Craft glue
- ⅛in (3mm) round wooden dowels

Tools

- Miter saw and box or craft knife and cutting mat
- Sanding sponge

MAKE THE PLANTER

1   Use a miter saw and box or a craft knife on a cutting mat to cut a 1½in (4cm) length of a paper or cardboard tube.

2   Trace the inner diameter of the paper tube onto a scrap of cardboard.

3   Cut out the circle of cardboard, insert it into the tube, and secure with glue.

4   Using a miter saw and box, cut about 30 1½in (4cm) lengths of wooden dowel. The quantity may vary depending on the diameter of your tube and dowels.

5   Apply craft glue to one side of each dowel and place them directly on the side of the planter until you have covered the whole surface.

6   Once dry, sand the planter as needed to create an even surface.

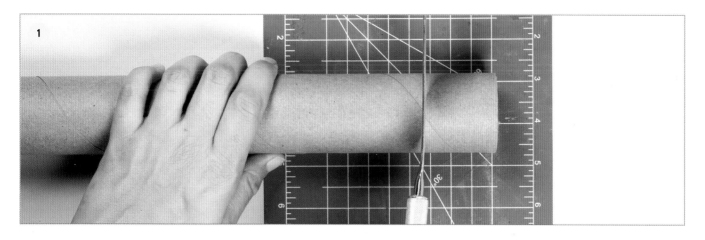

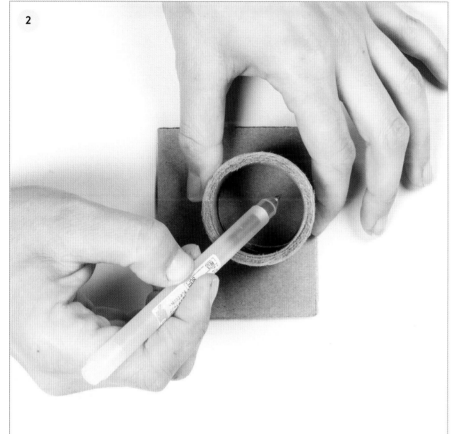

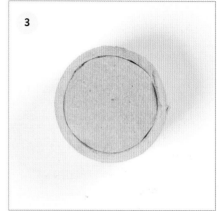

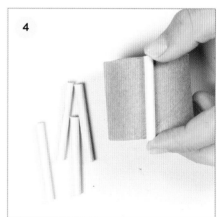

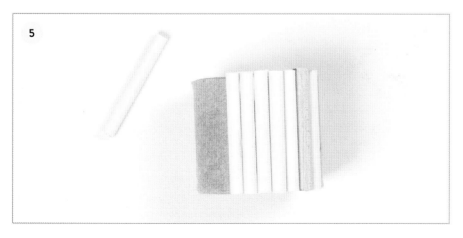

Dracaena Plant

A variety of heights in your dollhouse creates visual interest. One way of adding height is to include a tall indoor plant. This Dracaena uses some of the leaf-modeling techniques from the Sansevieria plant made for the living room – and a new technique for creating stems and branches.

Materials

- 16- or 18-gauge (1.3 or 1mm) bendable aluminum wire
- Kraft paper (or recycled paper bag) approximately 6 x 6in (15 x 15cm)
- Craft glue
- Dark green cardstock
- Light green acrylic paint
- Watered-down PVA glue

Tools

- Wire cutters
- Craft knife and cutting mat or scissors
- Fine paint brush
- Round wooden dowel
- Hot glue gun

MAKE THE PLANT

1   Using wire cutters, cut one 6in (15cm), one 5in (12.5cm), and one 4in (10cm) length of wire.

2   Tear the Kraft paper into strips ¼in (6mm) wide or less.

3   Apply a small amount of craft glue to one side of a strip and wrap it around each wire stem. Continue adding paper strips until all three stems are covered, applying more glue as needed. Allow to dry.

4   Use a craft knife or scissors to cut approximately 30 narrow leaves from dark green cardstock. They should all be less than ¼in (6mm) wide, but vary the lengths so that they are between 1 and 1½in (2.5 and 4cm). Bend each leaf gently around a wooden dowel to give it a slight curve.

5   Using a very fine paint brush, paint a light green stripe down the center of each leaf. When dry, apply a coat of watered-down PVA glue to each side of each leaf.

6   Beginning at the very top and working in a radial pattern, glue 10 leaves to each stem. Once dry, gently peel the outer leaves down to create volume.

7   Glue the completed stems into the planter using hot glue. Crumple the remaining Kraft paper to represent soil and use it to fill the planter.

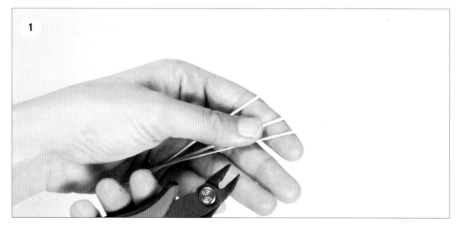

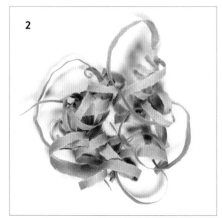

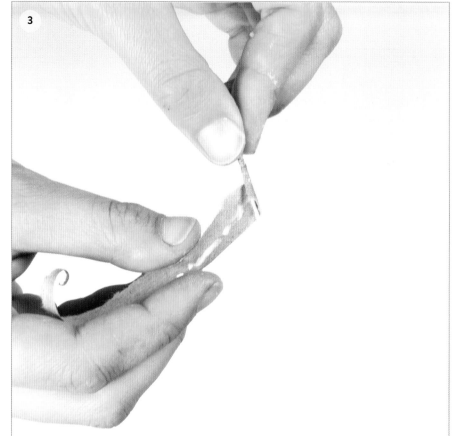

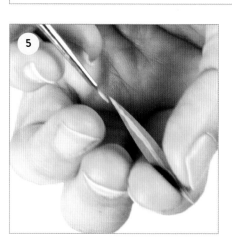

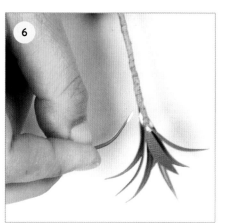

Painted Runner

With this technique, you will be able to make rugs with completely unique patterns and designs. Customize your rug by applying stencils or painting free-hand shapes for a more organic design.

Materials
- Aida cloth
- Heat-set fabric medium
- Acrylic paints in colors of your choice

Tools
- Fabric scissors
- Toothpick
- Pencil
- Paint brush
- Heat gun or iron

MAKE THE RUNNER

1   Use fabric scissors to cut a 2½ x 8in (6.5 x 20cm) piece of woven fabric such as Aida cloth (commonly used for cross stitch).

2   Use a toothpick to pull out horizontal threads from the last ¼in (6mm) of the rug's short sides to create a fringe.

3   On the top of the rug, use a pencil to outline a design. You can create wiggles, color blocks, or flowers; be as abstract or bold as you like.

4   For every color in your rug, create a mixture that is half acrylic paint and half heat-set fabric medium. Heat-set fabric medium prevents paint from cracking once dry and allows it to flex with the fabric. Paint these mixtures directly onto the fabric.

5   Once the paint is dry, set it by using a heat gun or by covering the rug with a clean cloth and applying a medium-hot iron.

Candle Holders

Tiny "candles" make this miniature dining room extra cozy. We're using toothpicks to replicate the tall look of tapered candles, with small stacks of stacked wooden beads for a set of modern-looking holders.

Materials

- 3 toothpicks
- Acrylic paints – white, black, and your chosen color for the holders
- White wax crayon or candle
- Wooden beads (approx. ¼in/6mm, any style)
- Craft glue

Tools

- Craft knife and cutting mat
- Paint brush
- Sanding sponge (optional)

MAKE THE CANDLE HOLDERS

1 Use a craft knife on a cutting mat to cut three toothpicks to between 1¼ and 2in (3 and 5cm) in length.

2 Paint the toothpicks white.

3 Once dry, coat each "candle" with a thick layer of white crayon or candle to give it a waxy appearance.

4 Add just a small dot of black paint to the tapered tip to represent the wick.

5 On the cut edge of the "candles", attach wood beads of varying quantities and styles to create a mismatched grouping. Secure each bead in place with a drop of craft glue.

6 Once dry, sand the base flat if needed and paint the beads in your chosen color.

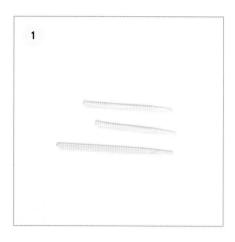

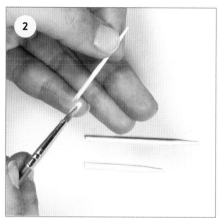

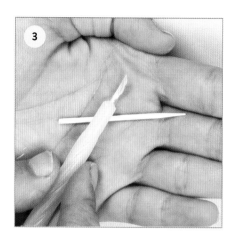

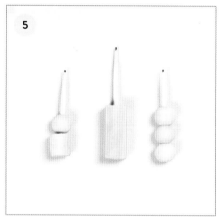

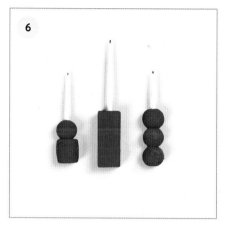

KITCHEN

Fridge Freezer

No kitchen is complete without a tiny fridge freezer. A taped hinge allows you to open and close the doors to fill it with tiny foods. Customize your fridge freezer by painting it in the color of your choice or make tiny "magnets" to adorn the outside.

Materials

- ⅛in (3mm) basswood sheet
- Wood glue
- Electrical or masking tape
- ⅛in (3mm) square wooden dowel
- Silver and white paints (acrylic or spray)

Tools

- Jeweler's saw or craft knife and cutting mat
- Miter saw and box
- Scissors
- Paint brush (if not using spray paint)

MAKE THE FRIDGE FREEZER

Refer to Templates: Fridge Freezer for details of what to cut.

1   Use a jeweler's saw or a craft knife on a cutting mat to cut parts A–G from a ⅛in (3mm) basswood sheet. Use a miter saw and box to cut parts H and I from a ⅛in (3mm) square wooden dowel.

2   Place part A on a flat surface.

3   Use wood glue to attach parts B and C around part A. Attach the B parts first (to the short ends), and then the C parts. Secure with masking tape until dry.

4   Attach part D 2in (5cm) from one end of the fridge.

5   Glue the shelves (E) into the larger freezer part of the opening.

6   Align the doors (F and G) on the front of the fridge freezer. Cut two small pieces of electrical or masking tape and attach them to the outside of the doors to act as the hinges.

7   Glue part H to the fridge door and part I to the freezer door.

8   Paint the fridge freezer inside and out in your color of choice. Spray paint will give you the smoothest and most even finish.

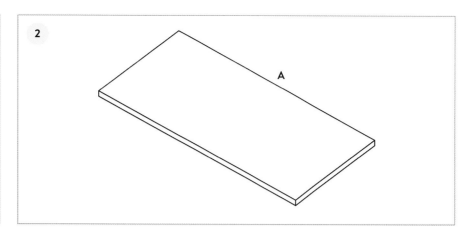

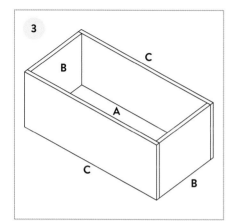

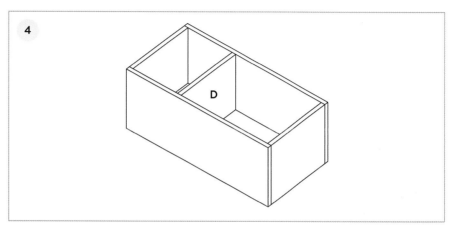

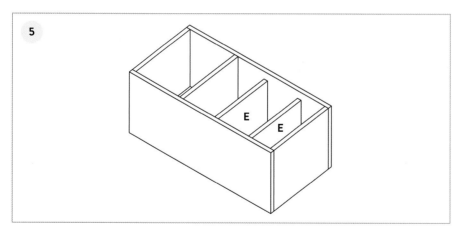

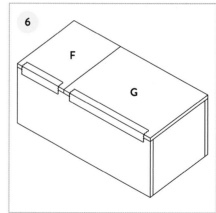

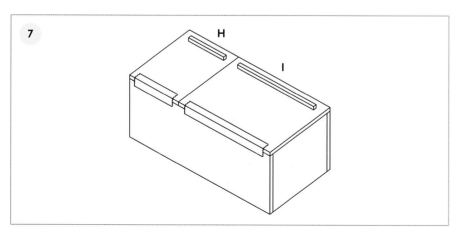

Stove

Functional elements in a dollhouse make it all the more fun. This miniature stove has an oven door that opens and shuts, and a piece of thin recycled plastic on the stove door allows us to look inside and see what's cooking.

Materials

- ⅛in (3mm) basswood sheet
- ¹⁄₁₆in (1.5mm) basswood sheet
- ⅛in (3mm) square wooden dowel
- Wood glue
- Fine surface filler
- Sheet of thin clear plastic (a recycled plastic food container works great!)
- Electrical or masking tape
- Silver and black paints (acrylic or spray)
- 4 small beads

Tools

- Jeweler's saw or craft knife and cutting mat
- Miter saw and box
- Scissors
- Paint brush (if not using spray paint)

MAKE THE STOVE

Refer to Templates: Stove for details of what to cut.

1 Use a jeweler's saw or a craft knife on a cutting mat to cut pieces A–D from a ⅛in (3mm) basswood sheet and piece E from a ¹⁄₁₆in (1.5mm) basswood sheet. Use a miter saw and box to cut pieces F–H from a ⅛in (3mm) square wooden dowel.

2 Use wood glue to attach the B parts to the top and bottom of the C parts to form an open cube. Allow to dry.

3 Aligning them at the base, glue the B/C assembly to part A.

4 Glue part D to the top of the B/C assembly. Once dry, fill gaps with fine surface filler as needed. Sand until smooth. Paint the exterior portions of the stove silver.

5 Create the oven rack by spacing the H parts equally between two G pieces and attaching them with wood glue. (If desired, paint the interior of the stove and the rack before connecting the two.)

6 Glue the oven rack in place.

7 Cut a thin piece of plastic to 2½ x 2⅜in (6.5 x 6.3cm) and glue it between the two E pieces. (If necessary to ensure that the stove stays closed, attach the remaining G part to the inside top edge of the oven door.)

8 Place the door on the front of the oven and cut a piece of electrical or masking tape to act as the hinge.

9 Close the oven door.

10 Attach part F to the front of the door as a handle.

11 Glue four small beads to the front of the stove and paint four black circles on the stove top to represent the burners.

2

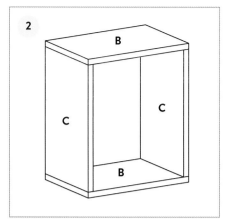

3

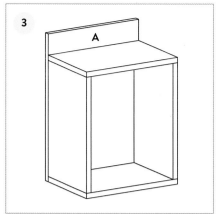

4

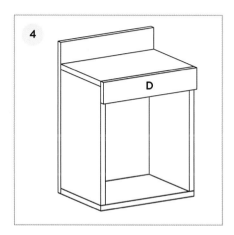

5

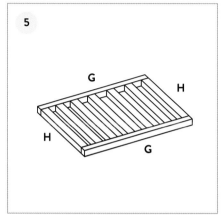

6

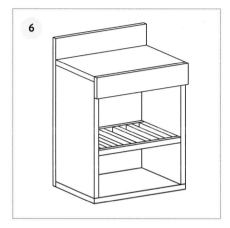

7

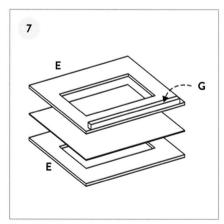

8

9

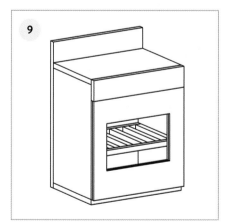

10

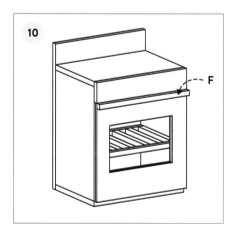

11

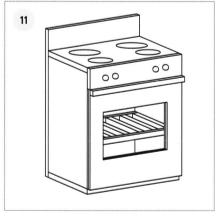

Kitchen Island

This miniature island works well as moveable counter space. Add stools to showcase the area as an eating space, or place the island against a wall to use it as a counter. Paint the counter in the color of your choice, or use the watered paint technique described here for a faux marble finish.

Materials

- ⅛in (3mm) basswood sheet
- White, gray, dark gray acrylic paints
- Watered-down PVA glue
- Wood glue
- Masking tape

Tools

- Jeweler's saw or craft knife and cutting mat
- Sanding sponge
- Paint brush

MAKE THE KITCHEN ISLAND

Refer to Templates: Kitchen Island for details of what to cut.

1 Use a jeweler's saw or a craft knife on a cutting mat to cut the pieces from a ⅛in (3mm) basswood sheet.

2 Sand parts A and B until smooth. Paint both sides of parts A and B white and allow to dry. Sand, and then apply a second coat of paint. Repeat this process until you are left with a smooth, consistent surface.

3 Thin a small amount of gray acrylic paint with a generous amount of water. Use a soft paint brush to create irregular veining to mimic marble stone.

4 Once dry, use a small paint brush to paint a thin dark gray vein over the previous streaks. Coat with watered-down PVA glue and set aside.

5 Using wood glue, attach the short side of the C parts to the short sides of part E.

Tip: *Use masking tape to hold the pieces in place to ensure the attachments dry at 90-degree angles.*

6 Attach the D parts to the outer edge of the assembly using wood glue.

7 Glue the two B parts to the outer edges of the counter assembly with the 4in (10cm) side pointing upward. Set aside.

8 Create the shelving unit by gluing the G parts evenly between two F parts. Secure with masking tape while the assembly dries.

9 Glue the shelving unit to the inner edge of one B part.

10 Glue part A to the top of the kitchen island.

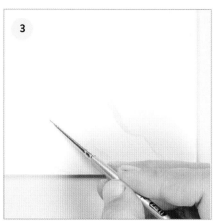

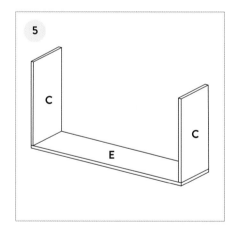

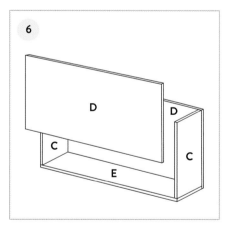

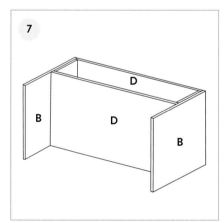

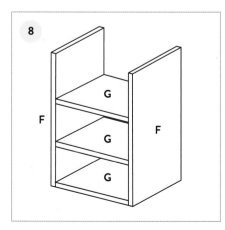

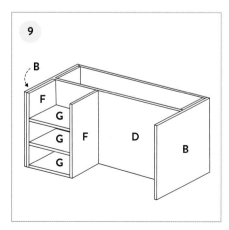

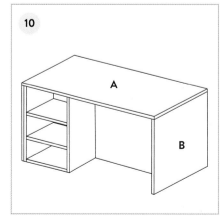

Fruit Bowl

Polymer clay is a soft and moldable material that can be formed into many complex shapes. For our kitchen, we'll keep the forms fairly soft to mimic handmade pottery. After creating this bowl, you might want to experiment with making miniature polymer clay fruit to fill it.

Materials

- Polymer clay
- Cornstarch (as needed)
- Acrylic paint (optional)

Tools

- Craft knife and cutting mat or clay cutter
- ¼in (6mm) round wooden dowel
- 1in (2.5cm) round wooden bead
- Oven
- Sanding sponge
- Paint brush (optional)

MAKE THE FRUIT BOWL

1 Condition your polymer clay by working it between your hands until it becomes soft. Then use a round dowel to roll the clay on a clean, flat surface until it is about ⅛in (3mm) thick.

2 Use a craft knife or clay cutter to cut a circle approximately 1¼in (3cm) in diameter.

Tip: *If the clay is too sticky, place it in a refrigerator to cool for a few minutes before cutting.*

3 Drape the clay circle over a small wooden bead or marble about 1in (2.5cm) in diameter. Use your fingers to gently press the clay over the form to create a bowl.

4 Remove the bowl from the form and bake it right side up in a standard oven at 275°F (135°C) for 12 minutes. When cool, sand gently as needed and paint if desired.

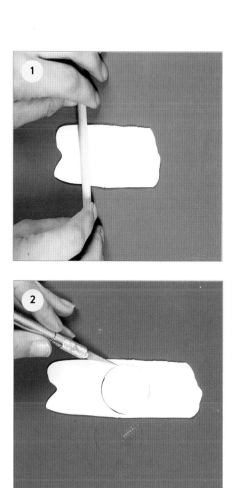

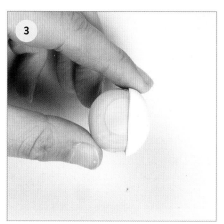

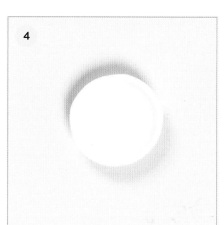

Plates & Mugs

Soft formed polymer clay plates are a nice homemade touch for use in both the kitchen and the dining room. Miniature coffee cups make every morning warm and cozy. Once baked, consider painting your creations with tiny decorative details.

Materials

- Polymer clay
- Cornstarch
- Acrylic paint (optional)

Tools

- Craft knife and cutting mat or clay cutter
- 1½in (4cm) metal washer, for plates
- 1in (2.5cm) round wooden bead, for plates
- ¼in (6mm) round wooden dowel, for mugs
- Toothpick
- Oven
- Sanding sponge
- Paint brush (optional)

MAKE THE PLATES

1   Condition your polymer clay by working it between your hands until it becomes soft. Use a round dowel to roll the clay on a clean, flat surface until it is about 1⁄16in (1.5mm) thick.

2   Use a craft knife or clay cutter to cut a circle approximately 1in (2.5cm) in diameter.

3   Place the clay circle on a large metal washer.

4   Place the washer on a flat surface, then press the wooden bead lightly into the center of the washer to create an indentation. Repeat on the underside.

5   Remove the plate from the washer and bake it right side up in a standard oven at 275°F (135°C) for 12 minutes. When cool, sand gently as needed and paint if desired.

MAKE THE MUGS

1   Condition your polymer clay by working it between your hands until it becomes soft. Use a round dowel to roll the clay on a clean, flat surface until it is about 1⁄16in (1.5mm) thick.

2   Use a craft knife to cut a rectangle approximately 1 x ½in (2.5 x 1.2cm).

3   Apply a thin coat of cornstarch to the end of a ¼in (6mm) round wooden dowel and gently roll the clay rectangle around it.

4   Use your fingers to close the seam.

5   Remove the mug from the dowel. Place the mug on a flat surface, drop a 1⁄8in (3mm) ball of clay into it, and use the dowel to flatten the ball into the base. Roll the mug along a flat surface to correct the shape as needed.

6   Roll a small piece of clay to 1⁄16 x ½in (1.5mm x 1.2cm) for the handle. Use a toothpick to attach the handle to the body of the mug.

7   Bake right side up in a standard oven at 275°F (135°C) for 12 minutes. When cool, sand gently as needed and paint if desired.

Tip: *If it's too difficult to remove the plate from the washer, bake the plate and washer together!*

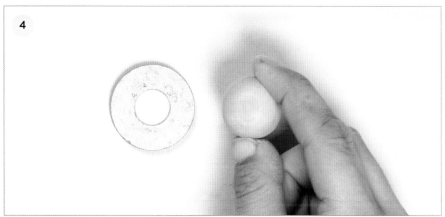

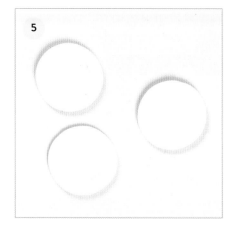

Tip: *Wash your hands frequently when working with polymer clay to prevent dust and dirt from damaging your project.*

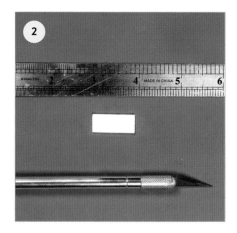

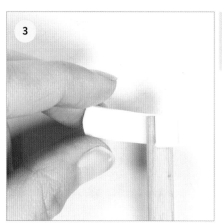

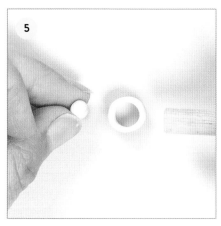

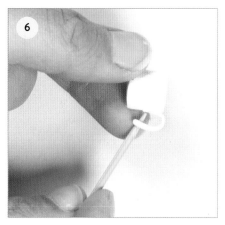

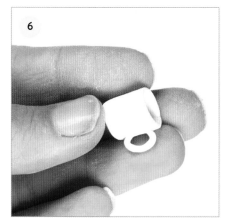

Plant Hanger

Add some green to your wall space with a bright and airy hanging planter. Customize the piece by painting the bead planter in your favorite color and adding a contrasting string. To hang it from the wall or ceiling, a pushpin, double-sided tape, or small eyelet would all work beautifully.

Materials

- Embroidery floss
- 1in (2.5cm) round wooden bead
- Craft glue
- Green craft paper
- Pushpin, double-sided tape, or eyelet/cup hook (optional—for attaching the planter to the wall or ceiling)

Tools

- Craft knife and cutting mat
- Round wooden dowel or paint brush

MAKE THE PLANT HANGER

1 Knot together the ends of six 10in (25cm) lengths of embroidery floss and attach them to a wooden bead with craft glue.

2 Tie knots between every two strings approximately ¼in (6mm) from the first knot.

3 Repeat this process to create three layers of knots, alternating strings for each layer.

4 Knot the strings together, ½in (1.2cm) from the end.

5 Use a craft knife to cut 10 leaves from green craft paper. Each leaf should be approximately ½in (1.2cm) long with a thin "stem" of about ½in (1.2cm).

6 Paint both sides of each leaf with watered-down craft glue. When dry, curve the leaves over a round wooden dowel or a paint brush handle.

7 Attach the leaves to the center of the bead with craft glue.

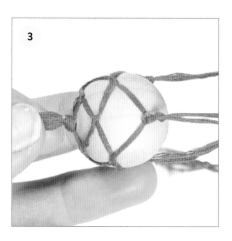

Tip: *It can be challenging to get all of your knots to align evenly. Double check the spacing of each knot before you pull it tight.*

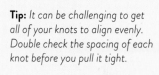

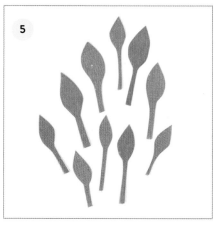

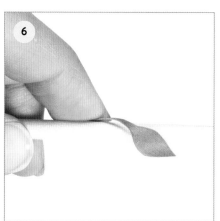

Kitchen Stool

Miniature kitchen stools are perfect as a side table or extra seat in any room. Pull them up beside the kitchen island for an easy eating nook. The angles of this design can be tricky, so be sure to use the gluing guide provided in the templates.

Materials

- ⅛in (3mm) basswood sheet
- ⅛in (3mm) square wooden dowel
- Wood glue

Tools

- Jeweler's saw or craft knife and cutting mat
- Sanding sponge

MAKE THE KITCHEN STOOL

Refer to Templates: Kitchen Stool for details of what to cut.

1 Use a jeweler's saw or craft knife on a cutting mat to cut piece A from a ⅛in (3mm) basswood sheet and pieces B–D from a ⅛in (3mm) square wooden dowel. Sand the corners of part A to give a slightly rounded edge.

2 Place parts B and C on the gluing guide (see Templates: Kitchen Stool). Apply glue to both ends of part C and attach it between parts B. Allow the assembly to dry on the gluing guide to ensure that the pieces dry at the correct angles. Repeat to create the second stool leg.

3 Glue the D parts between each leg to form the base of the stool.

4 Once dry, gently sand the tops and bottoms of the stool legs to ensure that they are level.

5 Apply a small amount of wood glue to the tops of the leg assemblies and carefully attach part A.

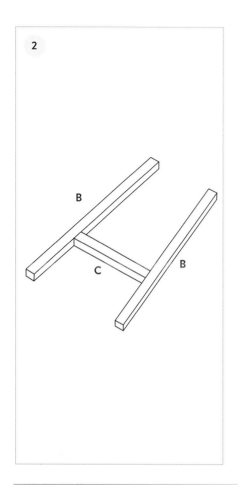

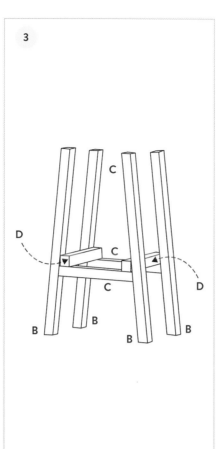

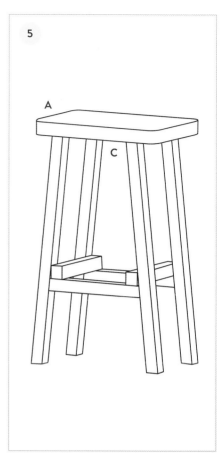

BATHROOM

Bathtub

A bright white faux-porcelain bathtub is the perfect place to unwind. To create this smooth shape we'll use foamcore and fine surface filler. The finishing touch is a bent wire faucet that even has handles that can really be turned.

Materials

- ¼in (6mm) white foamcore
- Masking tape
- Fine surface filler
- Spray paint (optional)
- Watered-down PVA glue (optional)
- 14-gauge (1.5mm) bendable aluminum wire
- Toy filling or cotton balls (optional)

Tools

- Craft knife and cutting mat
- Hot glue gun
- Sandpaper or sanding sponge
- Wire cutters
- Needle-nose pliers
- Pin vise and ¹⁄₁₆in (1.5mm) drill bit

MAKE THE BATHTUB

Refer to Templates: Bathtub for details of what to cut.

1 Use a craft knife on a cutting mat to cut the oval base from ¼in (6mm) white foamcore. In addition, cut a 2 x 12¾in (5 x 32.5cm) rectangle of foamcore and remove the paper backing from both sides.

2 Use a round object, such as a bottle of glue, to gently curl the foamcore rectangle.

3 Use hot glue to attach the piece to the edge of the oval base. Connect the two ends with a piece of masking tape.

4 Using your fingers, apply a generous coating of fine surface filler to all sides of the tub. Keep a cup of water on hand to smooth the coating as you go.

5 Once coated, allow to dry fully. Sand all edges using sandpaper or a sanding sponge.

6 Repeat this process until you have a smooth bath surface. If desired, spray paint the tub in the color of your choice, inside and out, and seal it with watered-down PVA glue.

Tip: *Foam doesn't like spray paint. Ensure that all the foam is completely covered with fine surface filler before coating it with paint or the foam will disintegrate!*

7 Use wire cutters to cut two 1in (2.5cm) lengths of wire. Bend each one in half.

8 Cut one 1½in (4cm) length of wire. Use needle-nose pliers to curve the top half into a hook shape.

9 Use a pin vise to drill three holes at one end of the tub.

10 Insert the longest wire into the center hole and the two shorter pieces into the holes on either side.

Tip: *Fill the tub with toy filling or cotton balls to give the illusion of a bubble bath.*

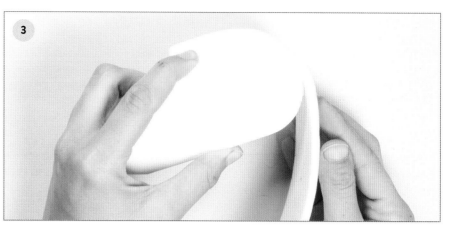

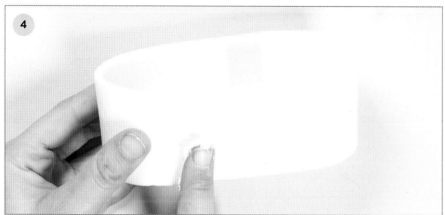

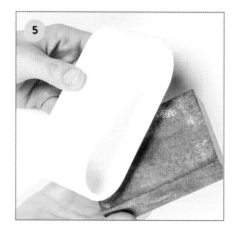

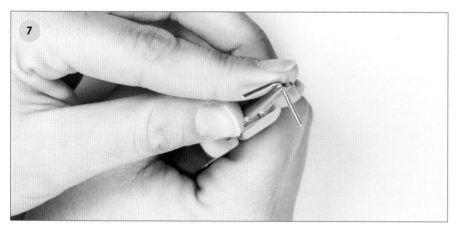

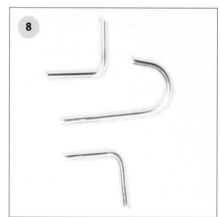

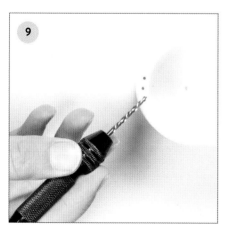

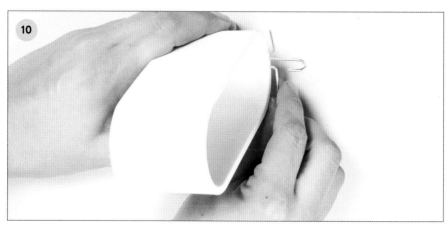

Toilet

No miniature bathroom is complete without a tiny toilet. The lid on this model even opens and closes using a tiny wire hinge. The modern silhouette is created using foamcore and fine surface filler to match the bathtub.

Materials

- ¼in (6mm) white foamcore
- Fine surface filler
- White spray paint (optional)
- Watered-down PVA glue (optional)
- 22-gauge (0.6mm) bendable aluminum wire
- Silver acrylic paint

Tools

- Craft knife and cutting mat
- Hot glue gun
- Sandpaper or sanding sponge
- Wire cutters
- Paint brush

MAKE THE TOILET

Refer to Templates: Toilet for details of what to cut.

1 Use a craft knife on a cutting mat to cut the pieces from ¼in (6mm) white foamcore.

2 Using a hot glue gun, connect both A pieces.

3 Hot glue part B to the center of the A assembly.

4 Hot glue part C to the tank resting on part B.

5 Gently curl part E and glue it to parts A and B.

6 Use your fingers to apply a generous coating of fine surface filler to all sides of the toilet, including part D. Keep a cup of water on hand so that you can smooth the coating as you go.

Tip: *Check that all the components fit together properly before coating with surface filler.*

7 Allow to dry fully. Sand all edges using sandpaper or a sanding sponge. Repeat this process until you have a smooth surface. If desired, spray paint the toilet white and seal it with watered-down PVA glue.

8 Once dry, align part D to the top of part C. Cut a 1in (2.5cm) length of wire and push it through to connect the components. Snip off any excess wire. Sand as needed to ensure that the toilet lid lifts up.

9 Paint a small silver circle at the top of the toilet "tank" to act as the flush.

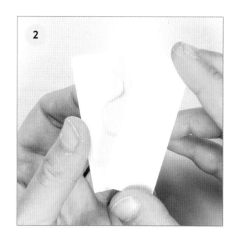

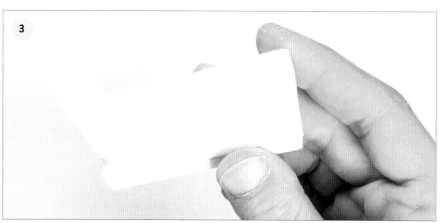

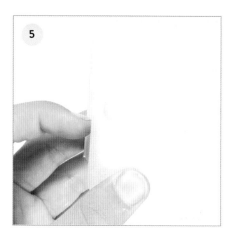

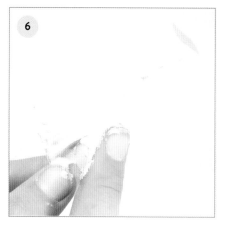

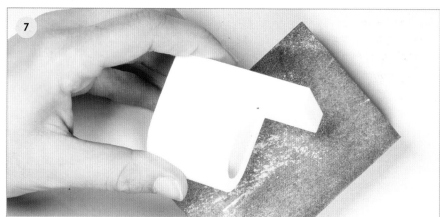

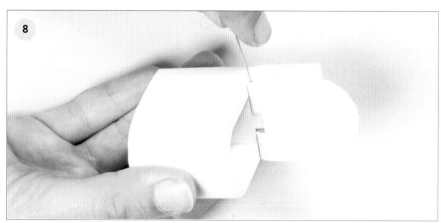

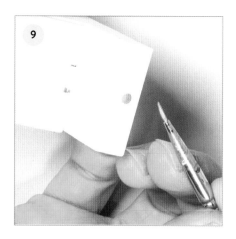

Sink

This foamcore sink has faucet handles that can be turned on or off. This sink basin sits beautifully on a wooden cabinet. Add details beside it, such as a small plant or hand towels, to customize the scene.

Materials

- ¼in (6mm) white foamcore
- Fine surface filler
- Spray paint (optional)
- Watered-down PVA glue (optional)
- 14-gauge (1.5mm) bendable aluminum wire

Tools

- Craft knife and cutting mat
- Hot glue gun
- Sandpaper or sanding sponge
- Wire cutters
- Needle-nose pliers
- Pin vise and ¹⁄₁₆in (1.5mm) drill bit

MAKE THE SINK

Refer to Templates: Sink for details of what to cut.

1   Use a craft knife on a cutting mat to cut the pieces from ¼in (6mm) white foamcore.

2   Using a hot glue gun, attach the two B parts to the short ends of part A.

3   Glue the two C parts to the remaining sides of part A to form a tray.

4   Use your fingers to apply a generous coating of fine surface filler to all sides of the sink basin. Keep a cup of water on hand to smooth the coating as you go.

5   Allow to dry fully. Sand all edges using sandpaper or a sanding sponge. Repeat this process until you have a smooth surface. If desired, spray paint the sink basin in the color of your choice and seal with watered-down PVA glue.

6   Use wire cutters to cut one 1½in (4cm) and two 1in (2.5cm) lengths of bendable wire. Bend the 1in (2.5cm) pieces in half, and use needle-nose pliers to curve the top half of the 1½in (4cm) piece.

7   Use a pin vise to drill three holes at one end of the basin.

8   Insert the longest wire into the center hole and the two shorter pieces into the holes on either side.

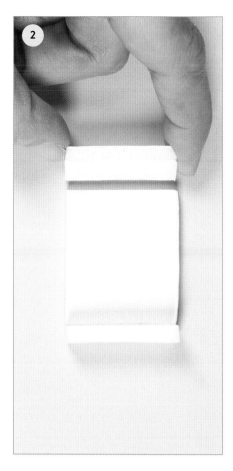

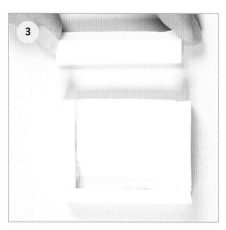

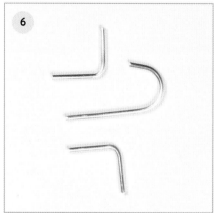

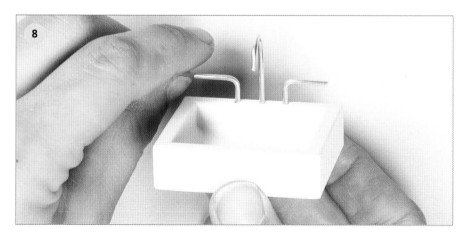

Tip: *Add a small dot of silver paint at the bottom of the basin to look like the drain.*

Sink Cabinet

This sleek and modern sink cabinet is the perfect place to store bathroom accessories. You can customize it further by applying wood stain. When it's complete, top it with your mini sink and fill the cabinet with mini towels and toilet paper.

Materials

- ⅛in (3mm) basswood sheet
- ⅛in (3mm) square wooden dowel
- Wood glue

Tools

- Jeweler's saw or craft knife and cutting mat
- Masking tape
- Miter saw and box

MAKE THE SINK CABINET

Refer to Templates: Sink Cabinet for details of what to cut.

1. Use a jeweler's saw or a craft knife on a cutting mat to cut parts A–D from a ⅛in (3mm) basswood sheet. Cut parts E and F from ⅛in (3mm) square wooden dowel using a miter saw and box.

2. Using wood glue, attach the long sides of the D parts to the short sides of the A parts.

3. Apply wood glue to the edges of the D parts and align part B to form a box. Secure with masking tape and leave to dry.

4. Turn the cabinet upright. Apply glue to the side and back edges of part C, then insert it into the cabinet as a shelf.

5. Apply one E part to each corner of the cabinet, aligning them with the top.

6. Use wood glue to apply the decorative F parts evenly between the cabinet legs. There should be six on each side.

7. Glue or place the sink basin on top of the cabinet.

2

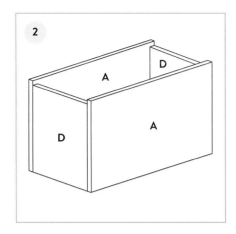

3

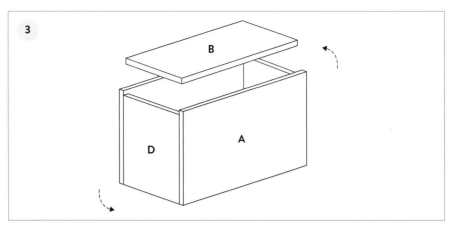

Tip: *With all the details in this cabinet, it may be easier to paint or stain the individual pieces prior to assembly. Just be sure to allow everything to dry fully before applying glue.*

4

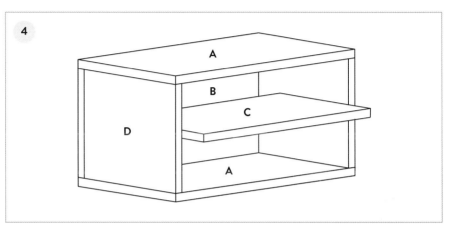

5

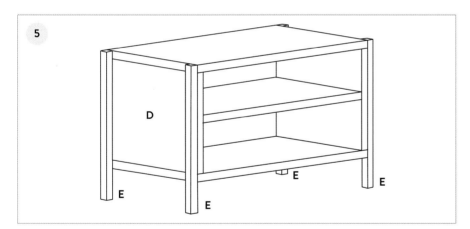

6

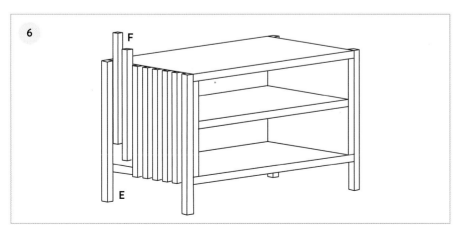

Bathtub Tray

Bathtime is even more relaxing when you have a bathtub tray to hold a book or a sweet-smelling candle. Paint or stain the final tray to add a splash of color to your miniature bathroom scene.

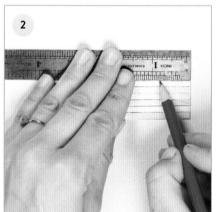

Materials
- ⅛in (3mm) square wooden dowel
- Wood coffee stirrers
- Wood glue
- Acrylic paint or wood stain (optional)

Tools
- Craft knife and cutting mat
- Pencil
- Ruler
- Sanding sponge
- Paint brush (optional)

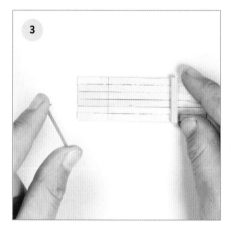

MAKE THE BATHTUB TRAY

1 Cut two 1in (2.5cm) pieces of ⅛in (3mm) square wooden dowel and six 3in (7.5cm) lengths of coffee stirrer.

2 Align the coffee stirrers and use a pencil and ruler to make a mark ¾in (2cm) in from each side.

3 Apply a small amount of wood glue to the square dowels and stick them over the pencil marks on the coffee stirrers. Sand as needed and paint or stain as desired.

Tip: *Check that the square dowels fit within the walls of the mini bathtub before you glue them in place.*

Towel Ladder

A ladder is a fun way to showcase colorful miniature towels. It utilizes vertical wall space to bring dimension to your tiny bathtub. Rest it against a wall beside the sink or bathtub. Customize it with your favorite wood stain or paint.

Materials

- ¼ x ⅛in (6 x 3mm) rectangular wooden dowel
- ⅛in (3mm) round wooden dowel
- Wood glue

Tools

- Craft knife
- Cutting mat
- Miter saw and box
- Pin vise and ⅛in (3mm) drill bit
- Pencil

MAKE THE TOWEL LADDER

1 Use a miter saw and box to cut two 5in (12.5cm) pieces of ¼ x ⅛in (6 x 3mm) rectangular wooden dowel and four 2in (5cm) pieces of ⅛in (3mm) round wooden dowel.

2 Use a pencil to mark the sides of the 5in (12.5cm) pieces at 1in (2.5cm) intervals.

3 Use your pin vise to drill ⅛in (3mm) holes in the rectangular dowels at the center of the pencil marks.

4 Insert the round dowels into the holes. Apply a small amount of wood glue if needed.

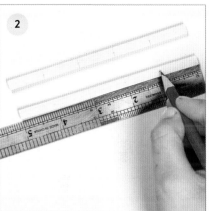

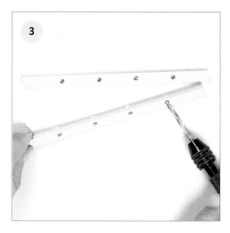

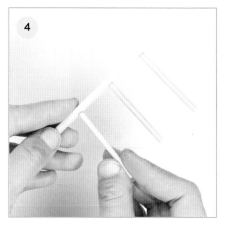

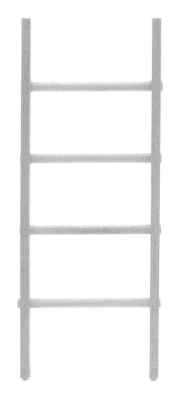

Twine Rug

This simple twine rug is a great bathroom accessory. Twine's warm color and rough texture mimic jute, a common rug material in full-scale homes. Play with different shapes, such as ovals or flowers, to customize it further.

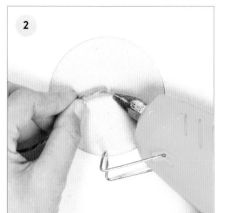

Materials

- Cardstock
- Twine

Tools

- Craft knife and cutting mat
- Hot glue gun

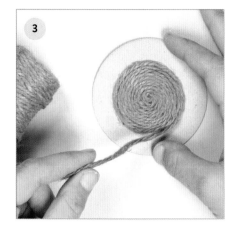

MAKE THE TWINE RUG

1   Use a craft knife to cut a 3in (7.5cm) diameter circle out of cardstock.

2   Place a small dot of hot glue in the very center of the cardstock and attach the end of your twine.

3   Wrap the twine around the circle to create a radial pattern. Apply small amounts of hot glue as you go to ensure that the rug holds its shape.

4   Trim the twine once you have covered the whole circle.

Towel

Bath towels are a fun and colorful detail to add throughout the bathroom. Fold several towels to stack below the sink cabinet. Drape additional towels over the towel rack and side of the bathtub.

Materials

- Terry cloth fabric
- Craft glue

Tools

- Fabric scissors

MAKE THE TOWEL

1 Cut a 1½ x 3in (4 x 7.5cm) rectangle of terry cloth.

Tip: Use the end seam of an old towel or rag.

2 Apply craft glue to one of the short ends and fold into thirds to close.

Alternatively: Hang the fabric over the towel ladder and apply glue to seal.

Tissue Box

A small tissue box is the perfect accessory for your sink cabinet. The box can be made from any color or pattern of cardstock as a decorative accent. The tiny tissue can even be removed from the box.

Materials

- Colored or decorative cardstock
- Craft glue
- Tissue

Tools

- Craft knife and cutting mat
- Metal ruler
- Coffee stirrer

MAKE THE TISSUE BOX

1 Cut a 1½ x 1½in (3 x 3cm) square of colored or decorative cardstock. Use a metal ruler and the underside of your craft knife to lightly score a ½in (1.2cm) grid on the paper.

2 Cut two pairs of parallel markings, as shown.

3 Cut the corner squares at a diagonal to create four triangular tabs. Cut a small slit in the center square.

4 Apply glue to the four triangular tabs and fold them over to form a box.

5 Cut an actual tissue into a 1in (2.5cm) square and use a coffee stirrer to gently push it into the opening of the tissue box.

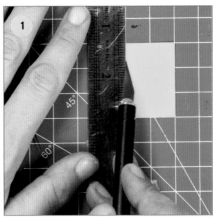

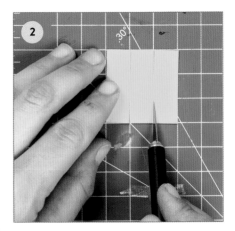

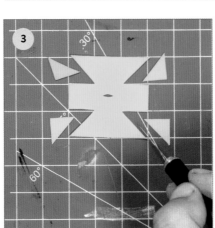

Toilet Paper

These miniature rolls are made from actual toilet paper and paper straws. They look adorable stacked on top of the toilet tank or stored in the sink cabinet.

Materials

- Paper drinking straw
- Toilet paper
- Craft glue

Tools

- Scissors

MAKE THE TOILET PAPER

1 Cut a ½in (1.2cm) length from a paper drinking straw and an 8 x ½in (20 x 1.2cm) strip of toilet paper.

2 Apply a small amount of craft glue to the drinking straw tube.

3 Gently roll the end of the toilet paper around the straw.

4 Apply a drop of craft glue ¼in (6mm) from the end of the toilet paper before fully rolling it up, or leave the end of the paper slightly unraveled to appear as though it's in use.

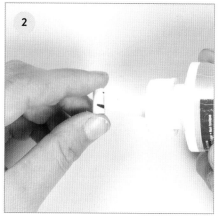

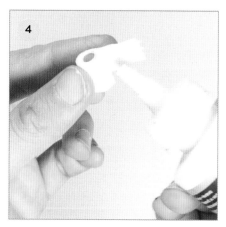

BEDROOM

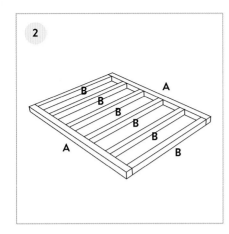

Bed

Get cozy with this sleek and simple bed frame. Made from square wooden dowels, it can easily be customized with paint or wood stain. Modify the width to make additional beds at varying sizes.

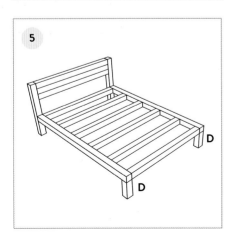

Materials

- ¼in (6mm) square wooden dowels
- Wood glue

Tools

- Miter saw and box
- Pencil
- Masking tape

MAKE THE BED

Refer to Templates: Bed for details of what to cut.

1   Use a miter saw and box to cut the pieces from ¼in (6mm) square wooden dowels.

2   Apply wood glue to the ends of six B pieces and space them evenly between the two A pieces. Allow to dry. Use masking tape to support the bed frame as it dries.

3   Glue the remaining three B pieces together lengthwise and attach them to the top of the two C parts. Allow to dry.

4   Use a pencil to mark both C parts ¾in (2cm) from the bottom. Apply a small amount of wood glue above that mark and secure the base of the bed frame to the backrest.

5   Glue the two D pieces to the opposite end of the bed base to create a level frame.

Mattress

No bed is complete without a mattress and the added detail of quilted tufts really brings this one to life. It's so cozy, you might just need to take a nap after making it! This mattress is hand sewn for durability, but feel free to use a sewing machine if available.

Materials
- Cotton batting or foam
- Cotton fabric
- Matching thread

Tools
- Fabric scissors
- Sewing needle
- Sewing machine (optional)

MAKE THE MATTRESS

1   Cut a 4 x 6in (10 x 15cm) piece of cotton batting or foam and a 5 x 14in (12.5 x 35.5cm) piece of cotton fabric.

2   Fold the cotton fabric in half lengthwise, with the patterned sides facing inward. Sew along both long sides ¼in (6mm) from the edge of the fabric. (You can use a sewing machine for this if you prefer.)

3   Turn the fabric right side out and insert the batting or foam.

4   Fold the remaining fabric at the open end inward and sew shut.

5   Thread your needle with a doubled length of thread and take the needle all the way through the center of the mattress, leaving a tail of thread about 1in (2.5cm) long. Take the needle back again, bringing it out right next to where you first inserted it. Knot all four thread ends together as close to the mattress as possible, then trim the ends to about ¼in (6mm) to create a tuft. Repeat the tufting process in all four corners of the mattress.

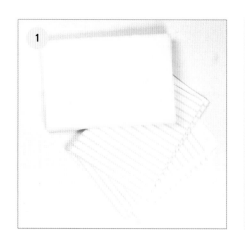

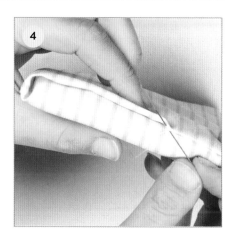

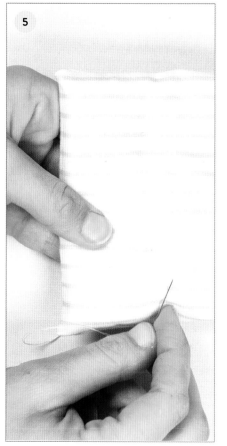

Pillows

Pillows are essential for a comfy, cozy bed. Start with two simple pillows for the head. You can make additional decorative throw pillows throughout your mini home using this same technique.

Materials
- Cotton fabric
- Toy filling
- Matching thread

Tools
- Fabric scissors
- Sewing needle
- Wooden dowel

MAKE THE PILLOWS

1 Cut a 3 x 3in (7.5 x 7.5cm) piece of cotton fabric.

2 Fold it in half, with the patterned sides facing inward, and sew the long side closed.

3 Turn the fabric right side out. Fold one end of the fabric inward and sew to close.

4 Use a wooden dowel to stuff the pillow evenly with toy filling.

5 Tuck the remaining end of the fabric inward and sew shut.

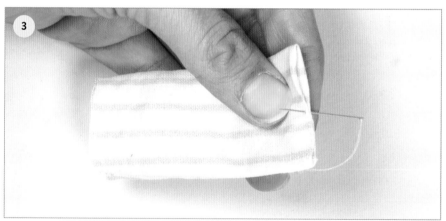

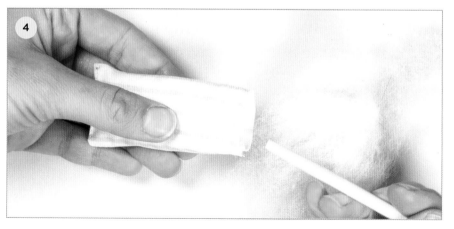

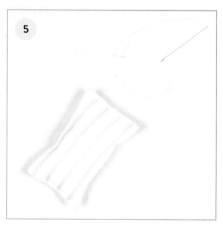

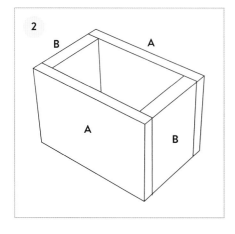

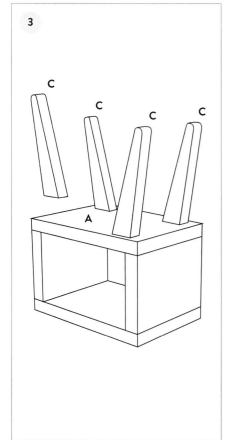

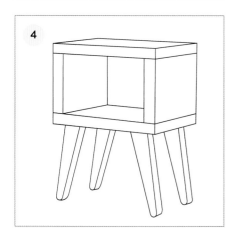

Bedside Table

This mini bedside table has the perfect nook to stash your favorite nighttime reading material. Consider making two so that you have a matching set for either side of the bed.

Materials

- ⅛in (3mm) basswood sheet
- Wood glue
- Acrylic paint in your chosen color (optional)

Tools

- Jeweler's saw or craft knife and cutting mat
- Sanding sponge
- Masking tape
- Paint brush (optional)

MAKE THE BEDSIDE TABLE

Refer to Templates: Bedside Table for details of what to cut.

1 Use a jeweler's saw or craft knife on a cutting mat to cut the pieces from a ⅛in (3mm) basswood sheet. Sand all C pieces to have smooth, rounded edges.

2 Apply wood glue to the long sides of both B parts. Align the short sides of the A parts to these edges. Use masking tape to support the structure while it dries.

3 Turn the table over onto its top. Apply glue to the wide end of the C parts and position them approximately ⅛in (3mm) in from each corner. Ensure that the legs taper outward.

4 Allow the table to dry upside down before turning it right side up. Paint if desired.

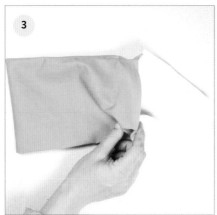
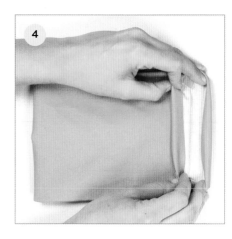

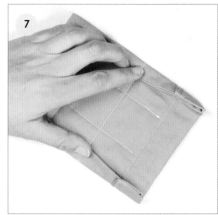

Quilt

A warm quilt is a great way to add color or pattern to your miniature bedroom. Detailed stitching makes the bedding more realistic. Ironing the quilt edges after assembly allows it to drape over the mattress more easily.

Materials

- Cotton fabric
- ⅛in (3mm) cotton batting
- Matching and contrasting thread

Tools

- Fabric scissors
- Sewing needle
- Sewing machine (optional)
- Iron

MAKE THE QUILT

1 Cut a 6½ x 15in (16.5 x 38cm) piece of cotton fabric and a 6 x 6in (15 x 15cm) piece of ⅛in (3mm) cotton batting.

2 Fold the fabric in half lengthwise, with the patterned side facing inward. Using matching thread, sew the long edges closed.

3 Turn the fabric right side out and insert the batting.

4 Fold the remaining fabric at the opening inward.

5 Fold and sew down the excess fabric to create a 6in (15cm) square quilt.

6 Using contrasting thread, sew straight lines across the fabric in both directions, stitching through all layers, to create a quilted grid.

7 Fold each side over by ½in (1.2cm) and use a medium-hot iron to crease.

Throw Blanket

A quick-and-easy throw blanket, made using the same techniques as our living room rug, adds a fun detail. Customize the blanket further by embroidering a delicate design, or embellishing it with small beads.

Materials
- Soft, woven fabric

Tools
- Fabric scissors
- Pencil
- Toothpick

MAKE THE THROW BLANKET

1 Cut a 5 x 6in (12.5 x 15cm) rectangle of a soft, woven fabric. On the wrong side of the fabric, draw a pencil line ¼in (6mm) from all the edges.

2 Using a toothpick, loosen the horizontal fibers between the pencil line and the fabric edge. Gently fray the edges of the fabric by removing one strand of thread at a time.

3 Fold the blanket in half and place it on the bed.

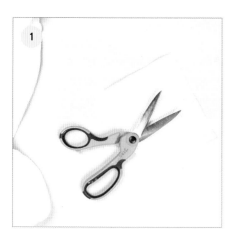

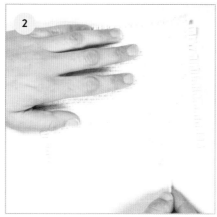

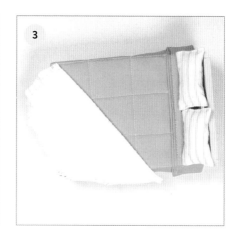

Table Lamp

This simple lamp looks perfect on your miniature bedside table. There are so many ways to customize it: you could skip the pleating for a smooth lampshade, paint the bead, or use the faux-concrete technique (see Techniques: Painting) to give the base a plaster-like texture.

Materials

- 1in (2.5cm) round wooden bead
- 1in (2.5cm) flat wooden bead or button
- ⅛–¼in (3–6mm) round wooden dowel
- Craft glue
- Colored paper

Tools

- Sanding sponge
- Miter saw and box
- Craft knife and cutting mat
- Metal ruler

MAKE THE TABLE LAMP

1 Sand the bottom of a wooden bead to give a flat base.

2 Find a dowel the same diameter as the bead's opening and, using a miter saw and box, cut it to 1½in (4cm) in length.

3 Glue the dowel to the center of the flat wood bead or button and allow it to dry.

4 Cut a 1 x 6in (2.5 x 15cm) piece of colored paper.

5 Use a metal ruler to fold the paper in opposite directions every ⅛in (3mm) to create accordion-style pleats.

6 Glue the ends of the pleated paper together to form a circle.

7 Apply glue to the edge of the flat wood bead or button.

8 Insert the bead or button into the paper lampshade. Allow to dry.

9 Apply glue to the round wooden bead's opening and insert the dowel.

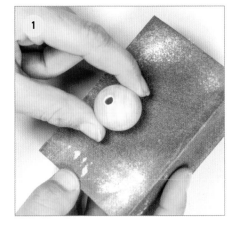

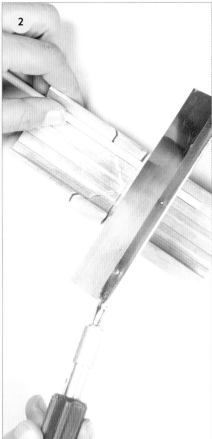

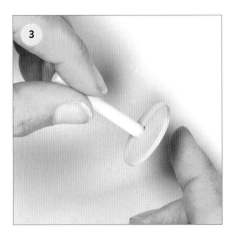

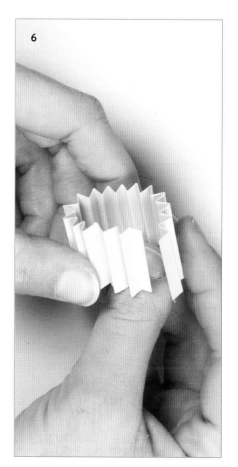

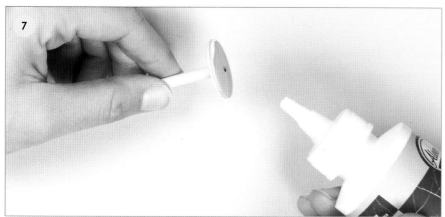

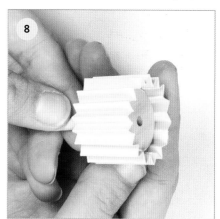

Clothing Rack

A folding clothing rack easily holds tiny hangers. It folds up for simple storage, but works as a great accent piece as well. Stock it with all your favorite fabric colors and textures.

Materials

- ⅛ x ¼in (3 x 6mm) rectangular wooden dowel
- ⅛in (3mm) round wooden dowel
- Wood glue
- Masking tape

Tools

- Miter saw and box or craft knife and cutting mat
- Pin vise and ⅛in (3mm) drill bit

MAKE THE CLOTHING RACK

Refer to Templates: Clothing Rack for details of what to cut.

1 Use a miter saw and box or a craft knife on a cutting mat to cut the pieces from ⅛ x ¼in (3 x 6mm) rectangular wooden dowel. Use a pin vise with a ⅛in (3mm) drill bit to drill holes through the A parts where indicated. Additionally, use a miter saw and box to cut a 3in (7.5cm) length of ⅛in (3mm) round wooden dowel.

2 Use wood glue to attach part B between two A parts, approximately ¼in (6mm) from the bottom of the angled side.

3 Use wood glue to attach part C between two A parts, approximately ¼in (6mm) from the bottom of the angled side.

4 Once dry, align the A/B assembly so that it is within the A/C assembly. The B and C parts should face outward. Align the pre-drilled holes at the top of the A parts, and insert the 3in (7.5cm) round dowel.

5 Gently push the dowel all the way through the second hole to connect the two parts. Open the clothing rack so that the angled edges of each A assembly are parallel with the ground.

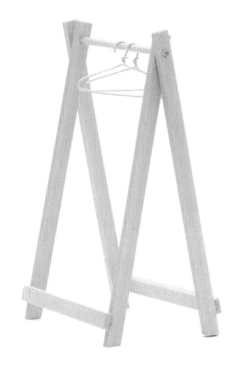

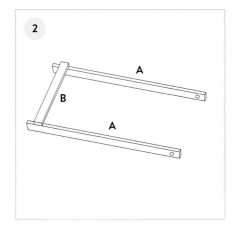

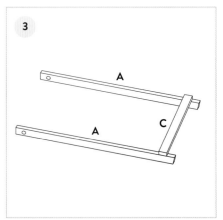

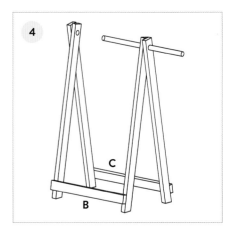

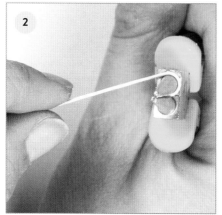
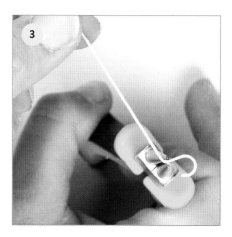
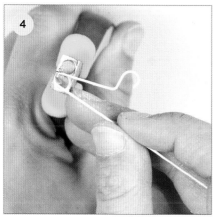
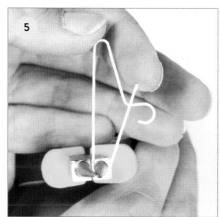
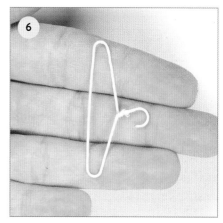

Clothes Hanger

Mini clothes hangers look so sweet on the clothing rack. The process is so fun and easy that you won't want to stop making them. Customize the color of your hangers with paint or colorful tape.

Materials
- 22-gauge (0.6mm) bendable aluminum wire

Tools
- Wire cutters
- Needle-nose pliers

Tip: *No mini clothing? No problem! Drape scraps of fabric over the hangers to give the illusion of clothing on the rack.*

MAKE THE CLOTHES HANGER

1 Cut a 4½in (11.5cm) length of wire.

2 Use the widest part of your needle-nose pliers to curl the end of the wire to create a hook.

3 Below the hook, bend the remaining wire in the opposite direction.

4 About ¾in (2cm) from the bend, curl the wire to form the first arm of the hanger using the middle of your needle-nose pliers.

5 About 1½in (4cm) from the first arm, curl the wire back toward the hook using the middle of your needle-nose pliers.

6 Twist the remaining wire around the base of the hook to close.

7 Trim off the excess wire.

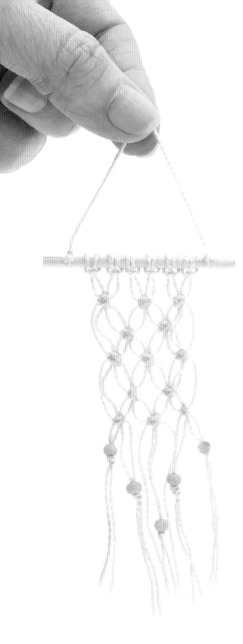

Wall Hanging

All it takes to create this calming macramé wall hanging is string and a small dowel – you can even use colored string to match your room decor. Add small beads for textural interest. A small piece of tape or a pin is all that is needed to attach this to a wall.

Materials

- ⅛in (3mm) round wooden dowel
- String
- Small wood beads (if desired)
- Masking tape

Tools

- Craft knife and cutting mat
- Scissors

PREPARATION

1 Cut a wooden dowel to approximately 2in (5cm). Cut six 12in (30cm) lengths of string.

2 Attach the string to the dowel using a lark's head knot. Fold the string in half and place the loop to one side of your dowel.

3 Feed the tails of the string over the dowel and through the loop.

4 Pull to tighten and repeat with all six strings.

CREATE A ROW OF THREE SQUARE KNOTS

5 Cross string #4 over strings #2 and #3 to form a "P".

6 Wrap string #1 over the tail of #4, behind strings #2 and #3, and pull it back through the loop created by string #4. Pull to tighten.

7 Take string #4 (now in the #1 position) and form a backward "P" over strings #2 and #3.

8 Wrap string #1 over the tail of #4, behind strings #2 and #3, and pull it back through the loop created by string #4.

9 Repeat this process for the remaining two square knots in this row.

CREATE A ROW OF TWO SQUARE KNOTS

10 Set aside strings #1, #2, #11 and #12.

11 Cross string #6 over strings #4 and #5.

12 Wrap string #3 over the tail of #6, behind strings #4 and #5, and pull it back through the loop created by string #6.

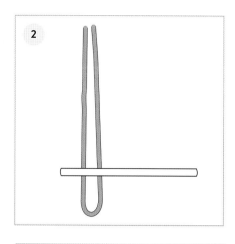

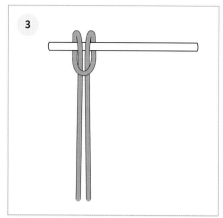

Tip: *Use masking tape to fasten the dowel to the table while you work on your knots.*

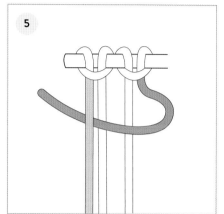

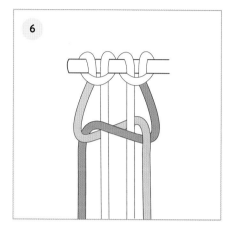

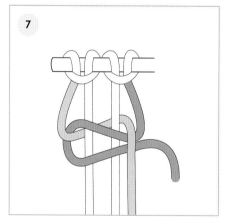

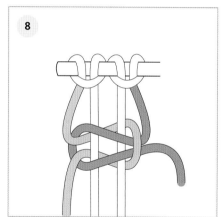

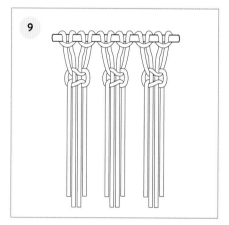

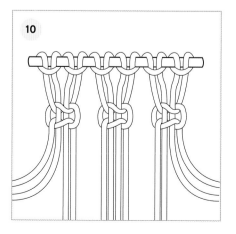

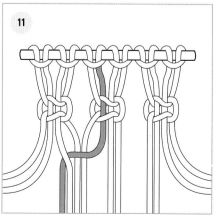

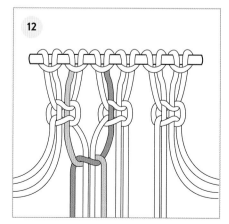

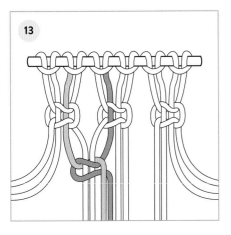

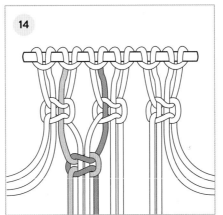

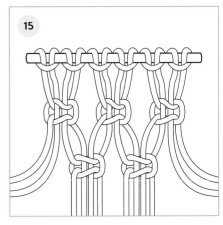

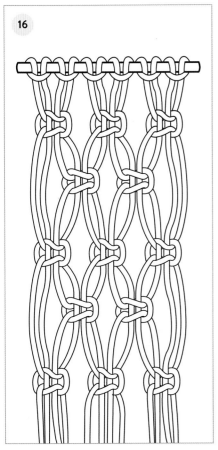

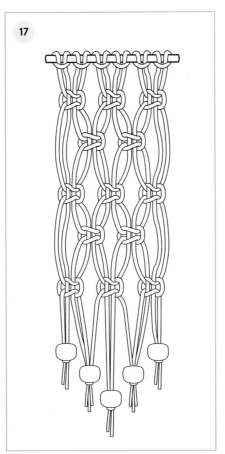

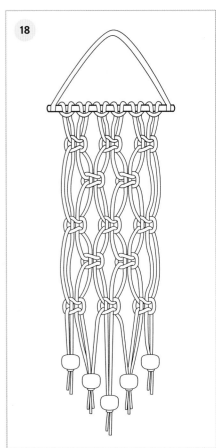

13 Take string #6 and form a backwards "P" over strings #4 and #5.

14 Wrap string #3 over the tail of #6, behind strings #4 and #5, and pull it back through the loop created by string #6.

15 Repeat this process for the remaining square knot in this row.

FINISHING

16 Continue making rows of three or two square knots until your macramé piece has reached the desired length.

17 Add a small wooden bead to the end of adjacent strings to weigh down the piece. Trim the strings to a neat taper as needed.

18 Cut a 5in (12.5cm) length of string and tie it to each end of the wooden dowel with a basic knot.

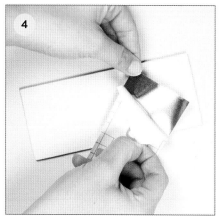

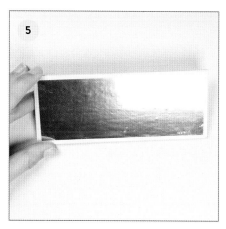

Mirror

With just two materials, this technique will allow you to make mirrors of all shapes and sizes. Experiment with different styles and you'll quickly have mirrors for every room in your dollhouse.

Materials

- ⅛in (3mm) basswood sheet
- Mirrored vinyl
- Acrylic paint (optional)

Tools

- Craft knife and cutting mat
- Sanding sponge
- Scissors
- Paint brush (optional)

MAKE THE MIRROR

1 Using a craft knife on a cutting mat, cut a 2½ x 6.5in (6 x 15cm) piece of basswood sheet.

2 Sand until smooth. Paint if desired and allow to dry.

3 Use scissors or a craft knife to cut a 2¼ x 5¾in (5.7 x 14.5cm) piece of mirrored vinyl.

4 Remove the adhesive from the back of the vinyl.

5 Apply the vinyl to the center of your mirror frame.

Tip: *Use a craft knife and cutting mat for rectangular mirrors, and a jeweler's saw for rounded mirrors.*

PATIO

Lounger

A classic wood lounger is great for a mini pool day. The backrest on this seat can be positioned up or down. For a splash of color, consider making a custom pillow or cushion using techniques from the bedroom furnishings chapter.

Materials

- ¼in (6mm) square wooden dowel
- ⅛ x ¼in (3 x 6mm) rectangular wooden dowel
- ⅛in (3mm) round wooden dowel
- Wooden coffee stirrers
- Wood glue

Tools

- Miter saw and box or craft knife and cutting mat
- Pin vise and ⅛in (3mm) drill bit

MAKE THE LOUNGER

Refer to Templates: Lounger for details of what to cut.

1 Using a miter saw and box or a craft knife on a cutting mat, cut pieces A, B, and F from ¼in (6mm) square wooden dowel and pieces C, D, and E from ⅛ x ¼in (3 x 6mm) rectangular wooden dowel. Also cut a 2½in (6.5cm) length of ⅛in (3mm) round wooden dowel, plus approximately seven 2¼in (5.7cm) and eleven 2½in (6.5cm) lengths of coffee stirrer.

2 Apply wood glue to the ends of two B parts. Attach them to the inside edge of the A parts to form a rectangle. Allow to dry.

3 Create a secondary rectangle by gluing together the two C and two D parts. Allow to dry, then place it inside the A/B assembly.

Tip: *The secondary, interior rectangle should fit snugly within the edge of the outer frame while still being able to move.*

4 Insert a ⅛in (3mm) drill bit in your pin vise and drill a hole through both rectangles on opposite sides of the lounger.

5 Insert the 2½in (6.5cm) length of round wooden dowel through the drilled holes.

6 Apply wood glue along one side of the E parts and attach them to the underside of the B parts.

7 Glue the F parts upright to the corners of the lounger, where the A parts meet the E parts.

8 Once dry, check that the chair hinge can move freely.

9 Use wood glue to attach approximately seven 2¼in (5.7cm) lengths of coffee stirrer to the chair backrest, spacing them evenly. Use wood glue to attach approximately eleven 2½in (6.5cm) lengths of coffee stirrer to the chair base, again spacing them evenly.

2

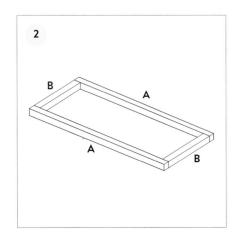

3

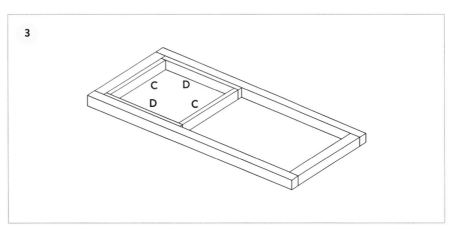

4

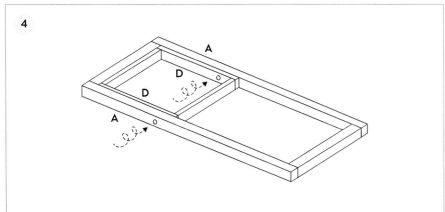

5

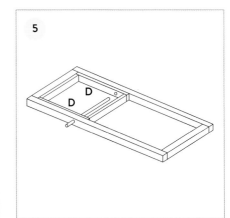

6

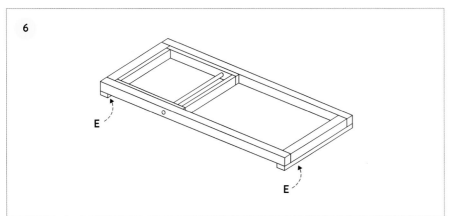

7

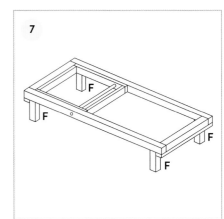

8

9

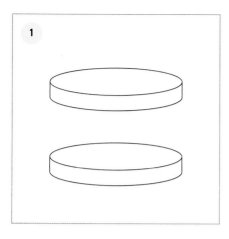

Side Table

Paint this mini side table for a pop of color. A mini side table is the perfect place for small plants and tiny beverages. Use the same design to create side tables wherever they are needed in the mini home.

Materials

- ⅛in (3mm) basswood sheet
- ⅛in (3mm) round wooden dowel
- Wood glue

Tools

- Jeweler's saw
- Sanding sponge
- Pin vise and ⅛in (3mm) drill bit
- Miter saw and box
- Metal ruler

MAKE THE SIDE TABLE

1 Use a jeweler's saw to cut two 1¼in (3cm) diameter circles from a ⅛in (3mm) basswood sheet. Use a sanding sponge to round the edges.

2 Stack the circles and drill four ⅛in (3mm) holes, evenly spaced.

3 Use a miter saw and box to cut four 1½in (4cm) lengths of ⅛in (3mm) round wooden dowel. Insert the dowels through both circles.

4 Adjust the spacing of the circles and make sure they're level – the dowels should be level with the top of the table and the shelf should be about ½in (1.2cm) up from the bottom of the legs. Add a small amount of wood glue if needed to secure the table top and shelf in position.

5 Sand the base as needed to create a level table surface.

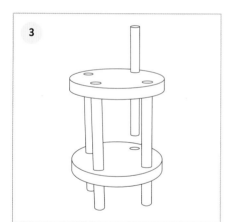

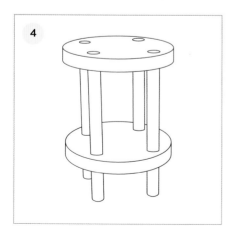

Sling Chair

These classic sling chairs are perfect for the patio. The soft fabric seat is a great place to experiment with colorful vibrant patterns. A dowel hinge allows this chair to open and fold like a true beach chair.

Materials

- ¼in (6mm) square wooden dowel
- ⅛in (3mm) square wooden dowel
- ⅛in (3mm) round wooden dowel
- Wood glue
- Cotton fabric
- Craft glue

Tools

- Miter saw and box or craft knife and cutting mat
- Pin vise and ⅛in (3mm) drill bit
- Sanding sponge
- Fabric scissors
- Binder clips

MAKE THE SLING CHAIR

Refer to Templates: Sling Chair for details of what to cut.

1 Using a miter saw and box or a craft knife on a cutting mat, cut pieces A–C from square wooden dowels. You will also need to cut three 2½in (6.5cm) and two 2in (5cm) lengths of ⅛in (3mm) round wooden dowel. Using a pin vise and a ⅛in (3mm) bit, drill holes in the A and B pieces where indicated on the templates.

2 Apply a small amount of wood glue to the end holes of the A parts and insert two 2½in (6.5cm) of the round wooden dowels to connect the pieces. Allow to dry.

3 Connect the two B parts in the same way, using the two 2in (5cm) lengths of the round wooden dowels.

4 Set the smaller rectangle within the larger one and align the remaining predrilled center holes.

5 Insert the remaining 2½in (6.5cm) length of the round wooden dowel to connect the two components.

6 Use a small amount of wood glue to attach part C to parts A just below the center round dowel.

7 Open the chair by rotating the smaller rectangle until it rests on part C.

8 Cut a 1½ x 5½in (4 x 14cm) piece of cotton fabric. Fold one end over the top of the chair and the other end over the seat. Use craft glue to secure the fabric and binder clips to hold the fabric in place as it dries.

2

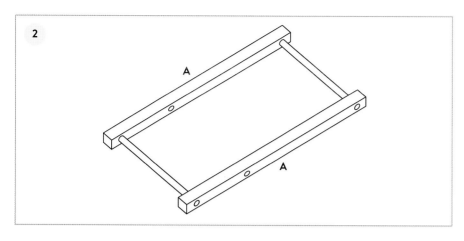

A

A

3

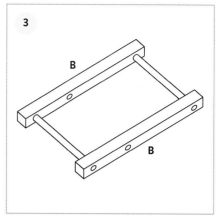

B

B

4

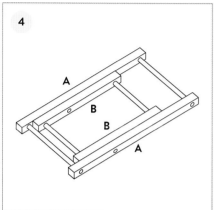

A

B

B

A

5

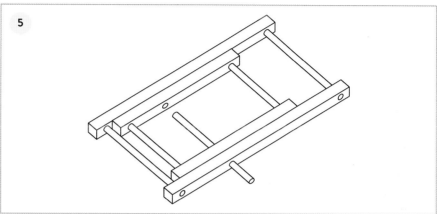

6

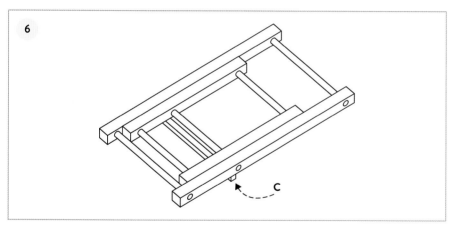

C

7

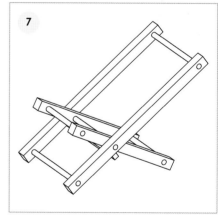

8

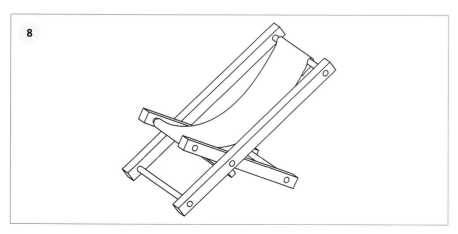

Tip: *Before you secure the fabric with glue, check that you can still open and close the chair fully.*

Tall Planter

This terracotta planter makes use of a recycled cardboard tube. The deep orange color brings a bit of warmth to your patio. The added detail of the wooden plant stand makes this feature even more prominent.

Materials

- Cardboard tube
- Scrap cardboard
- ⅛in (3mm) square wooden dowel
- ⅛ x ¼in (3 x 6mm) rectangular wooden dowel
- Wood glue
- Terracotta-colored and dark gray acrylic paints

Tools

- Miter saw and box or craft knife and cutting mat
- Paint brush

MAKE THE PLANTER

1 Use a miter saw or a craft knife on a cutting mat to cut a 1½in (4cm) length of cardboard tube.

2 Trace the inner diameter of the paper tube onto a scrap of cardboard.

3 Cut out the circle of cardboard, insert it into the tube, and secure with glue.

4 Create the faux concrete paint (see Techniques: Painting) using terracotta-colored paints rather than gray. Apply the mixture to all sides of the planter. Be sure to cover the bottom and inner rim of the planter.

5 Once dry, use a dry brush technique (see Techniques: Painting) to apply a small amount of dark gray paint to the faux terracotta surface.

6 For the plant stand, cut the following lengths of ⅛in (3mm) square wooden dowel: four 1½in (4cm) lengths, one 1⅛in (2.8cm) length or equal to the diameter of your planter, and two ½in (1.2cm) lengths or equal to half the diameter of your planter.

7 Glue the 1⅛in (2.8cm) piece between the two ½in (1.2cm) pieces to form a "+". Allow to dry.

8 Glue two of the 1½in (4cm) pieces to two opposite ends of the "+". Ensure that the two legs are level.

9 Glue the remaining 1½in (4cm) pieces to the ends of the ½in (1.2cm) pieces.

Tip: *The dimensions of your plant stand should vary depending on the final dimensions of your planter. Be sure to measure the diameter of your planter and adjust the stand accordingly!*

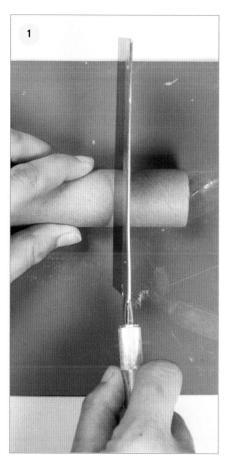

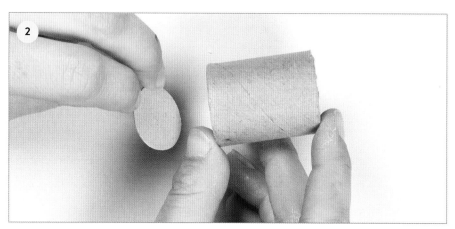

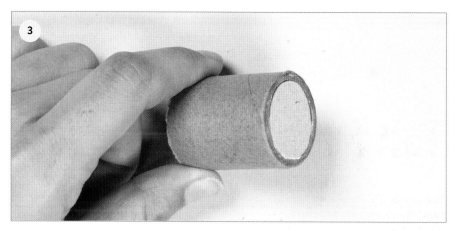

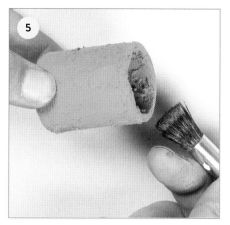

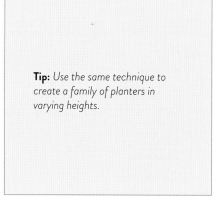

Tip: *Use the same technique to create a family of planters in varying heights.*

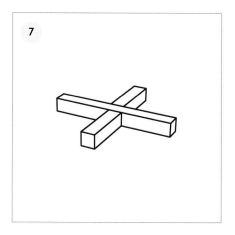

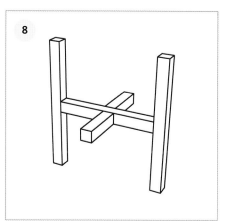

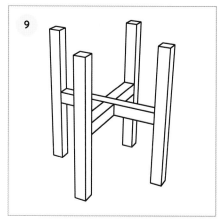

Palm Plant

A big palm tree brings color and texture to both indoor and outdoor mini spaces. To create these palm fronds we'll use several techniques from other plants in the book. The added step of attaching wire to each leaf provides a bit more stability and ensures that the leaves hold their shape.

Materials

- Green cardstock
- 16- or 18-gauge (1.3 or 1mm) bendable aluminum wire
- Craft glue
- Light green acrylic paint
- Watered-down PVA glue
- Scraps of packing foam
- Brown Kraft paper

Tools

- Craft knife and cutting mat
- Wire cutter
- Fine paint brush
- Scissors

MAKE THE PALM PLANT

Refer to Templates: Palm Plant.

1   Use a craft knife on a cutting mat to cut five leaves from green cardstock.

2   Cut five 6in (15cm) lengths of wire and attach one to the center of each leaf using craft glue. Allow to dry fully.

3   Use a fine paint brush to add a light green accent line along the wire and down each leaf. Repeat for the opposite side of the leaf.

4   Coat both sides of the leaves with watered-down PVA glue and allow to dry.

5   Gently curl and shape each leaf around a round dowel or tube.

6   Insert scrap packing foam into the planter.

7   Insert the wire stems of the leaves into the foam using glue to secure as needed.

8   Fill the planter with crumpled pieces of brown Kraft paper to mimic soil.

Tip: *Trim the leaf wire at different lengths to create variety in your leaf height.*

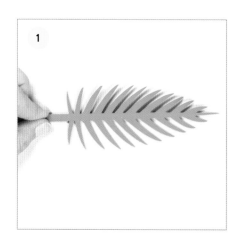

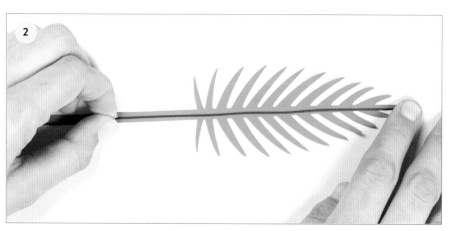

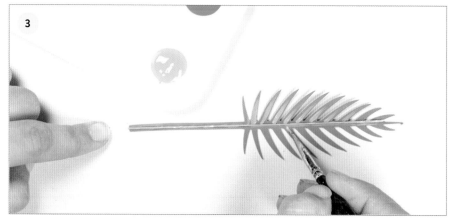

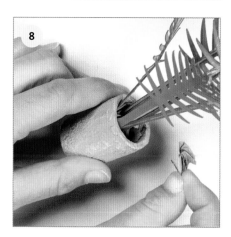

Templates

Templates are shown at actual size. All solid lines are cutting lines; broken lines are fold lines; and circles indicate where holes are to be drilled. Printable versions of these templates can be downloaded from www.davidandcharles.com.

Living Room

SOFA STRUCTURE

⅛in (3mm) basswood sheet

5½in (14cm)

E x 1

2¾in (7cm)

¼in (6mm) square wooden dowel

2in (5cm)

A x 2

2¼in (5.7cm)

B x 4

2½in (6.5cm)

C x 2

5½in (14cm)

D x 4

SOFA CUSHIONS

Seat cushion cover

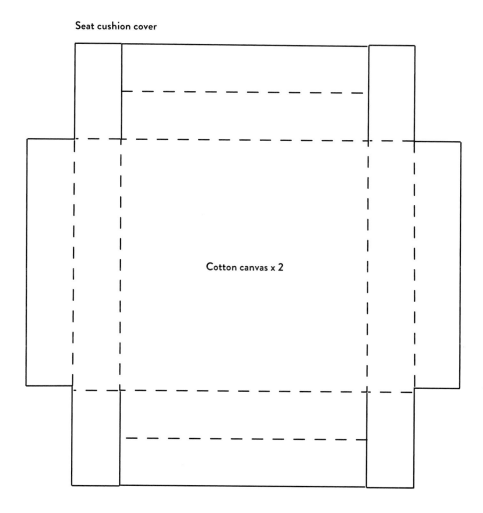

Cotton canvas x 2

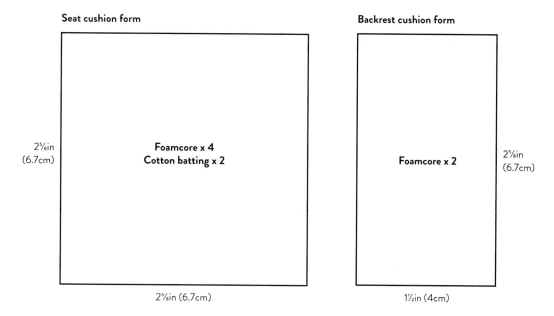

Seat cushion form

Foamcore x 4
Cotton batting x 2

2⅝in
(6.7cm)

2⅝in (6.7cm)

Backrest cushion form

Foamcore x 2

2⅝in
(6.7cm)

1½in (4cm)

BOOKSHELF

¼in (6mm) square wooden dowel

4¾in (12cm)

A x 2

¾in (2cm)

B x 2

5in (12.5cm)

C x 2

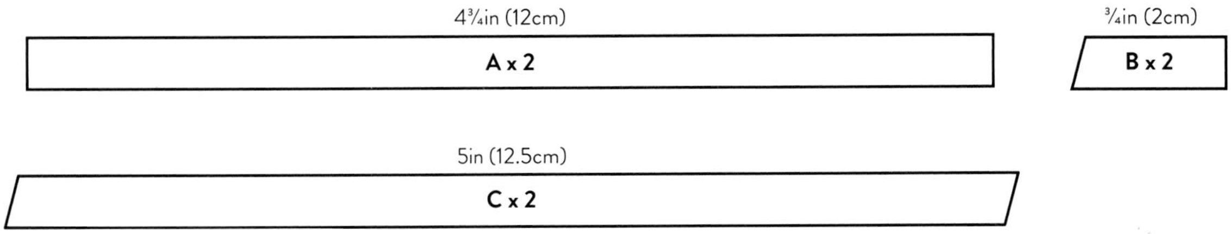

⅛in (3mm) basswood sheet

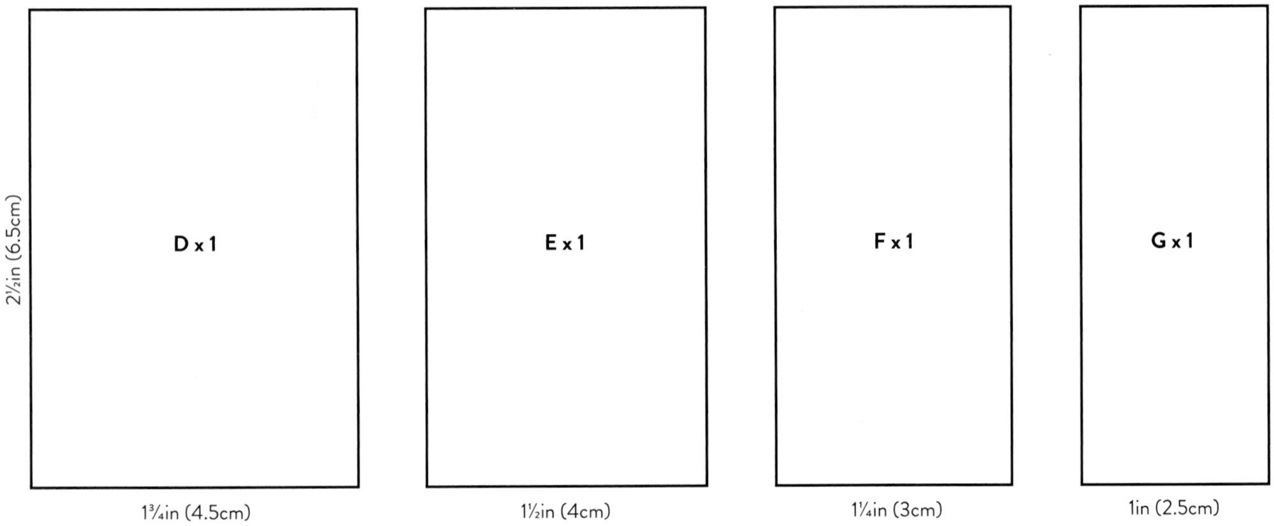

2½in (6.5cm)

D x 1

E x 1

F x 1

G x 1

1¾in (4.5cm)

1½in (4cm)

1¼in (3cm)

1in (2.5cm)

LOUNGE CHAIR

¼in (6mm) square wooden dowel

1in (2.5cm)

A x 2

2in (5cm)

D x 2

2½in (6.5cm)

B x 2

2½in (6.5cm)

E x 3

2¼in (5.7cm)

C x 2

2in (5cm)

F x 1

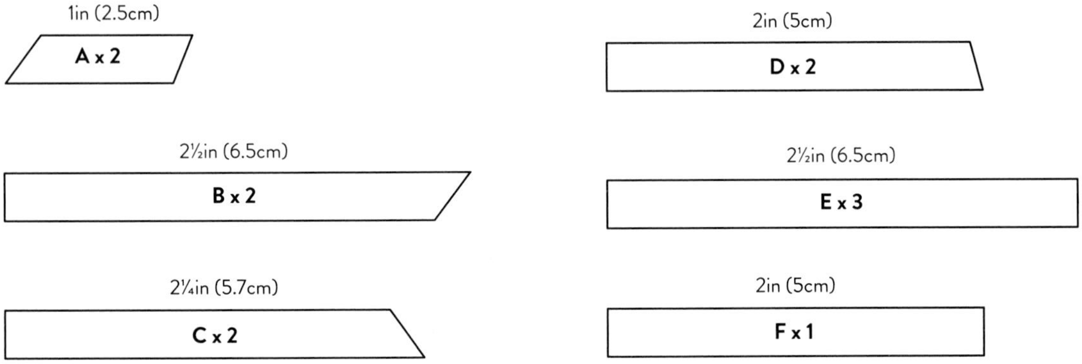

LOUNGE CHAIR

Waxed faux-leather paper or cotton fabric

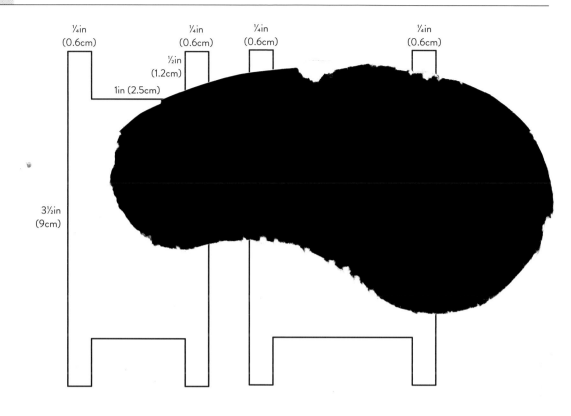

¼in (0.6cm)

¼in (0.6cm)

½in (1.2cm)

1in (2.5cm)

¼in (0.6cm)

¼in (0.6cm)

3½in (9cm)

LAMP

⅛in (3mm) basswood sheet

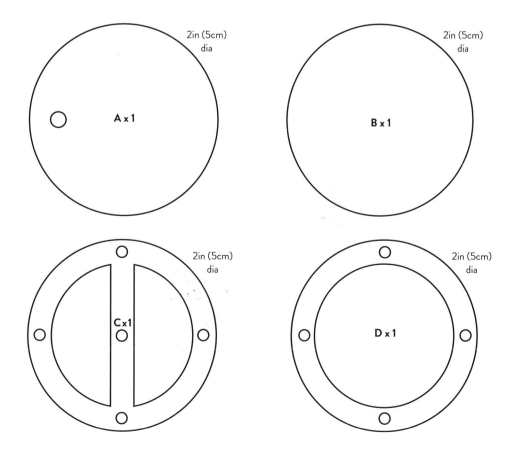

2in (5cm) dia

A x 1

2in (5cm) dia

B x 1

2in (5cm) dia

C x1

2in (5cm) dia

D x 1

⅛in (3mm) basswood sheet

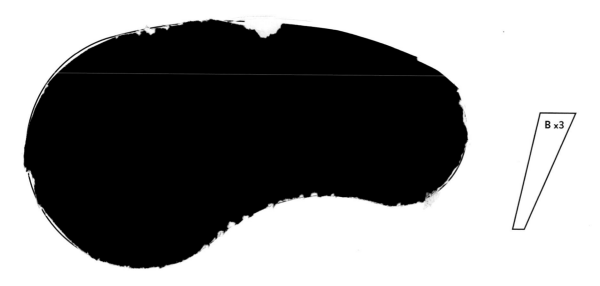

B x3

Dining Room

DINING TABLE

⅛in (3mm) basswood sheet

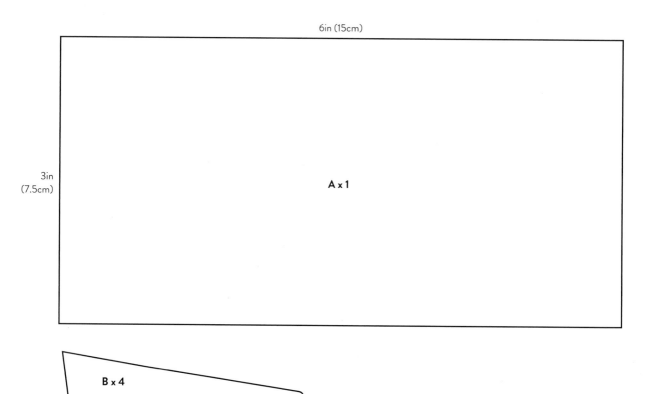

6in (15cm)

3in
(7.5cm)

A x 1

B x 4

DINING CHAIR

⅛in (3mm) basswood sheet

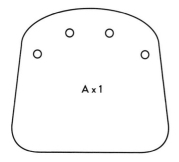

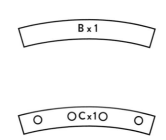

Kitchen

⅛in (3mm) basswood sheet

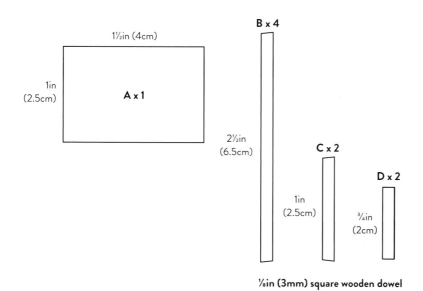

⅛in (3mm) square wooden dowel

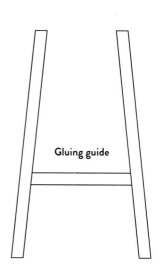

⅛in (3mm) basswood sheet

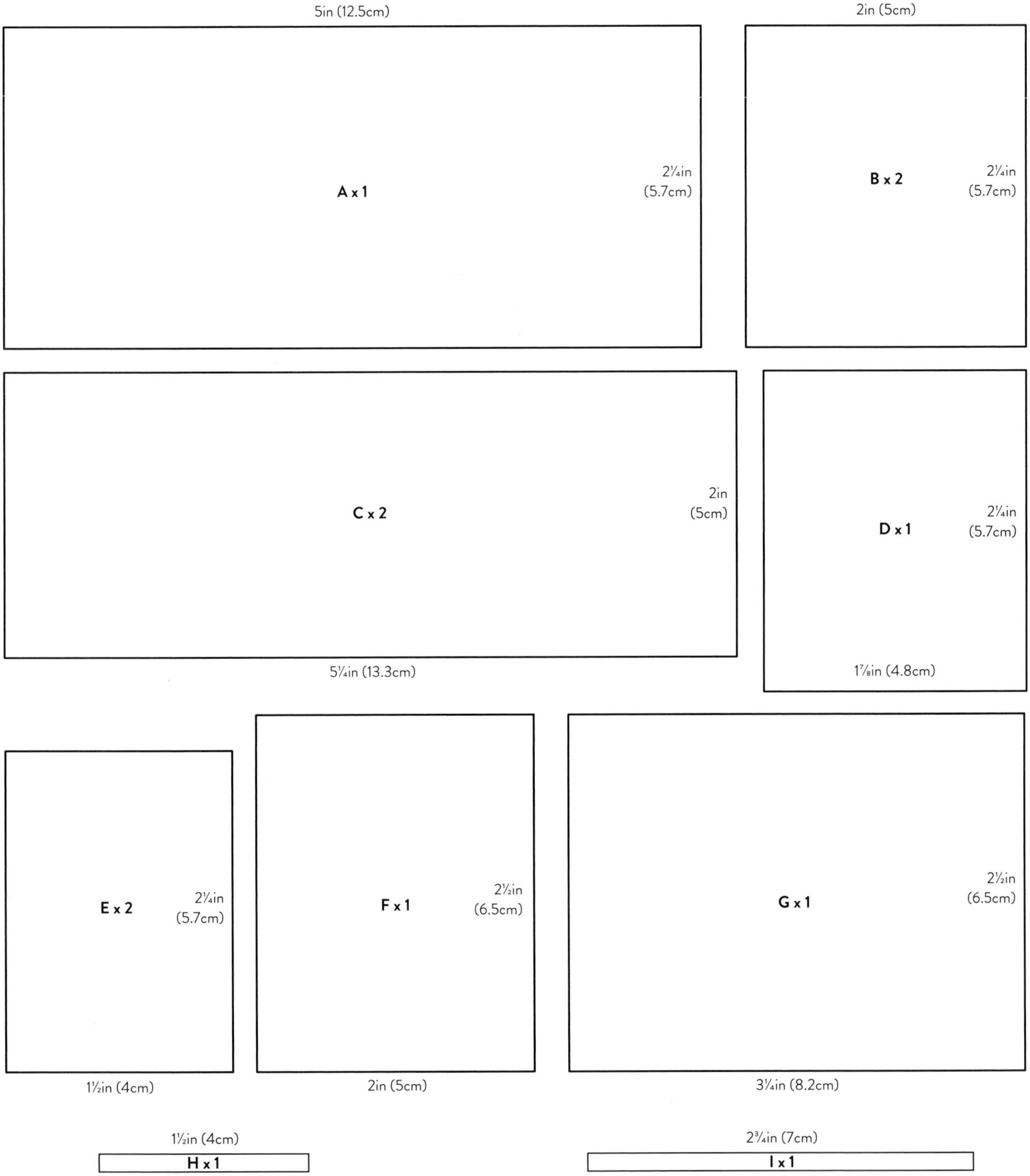

5in (12.5cm)

A x 1   2¼in (5.7cm)

2in (5cm)

B x 2   2¼in (5.7cm)

C x 2   2in (5cm)

5¼in (13.3cm)

D x 1   2¼in (5.7cm)

1⅞in (4.8cm)

E x 2   2¼in (5.7cm)

1½in (4cm)

F x 1   2½in (6.5cm)

2in (5cm)

G x 1   2½in (6.5cm)

3¼in (8.2cm)

1½in (4cm)

H x 1

2¾in (7cm)

I x 1

⅛in (3mm) basswood sheet

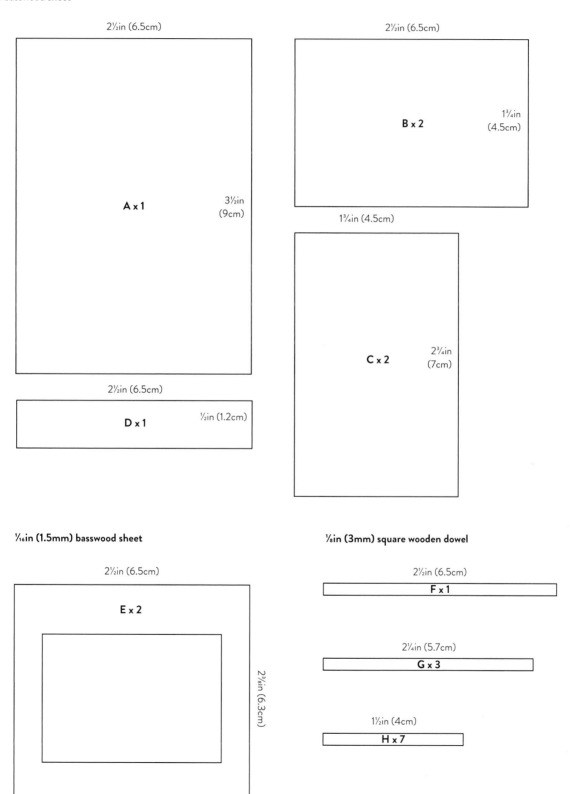

2½in (6.5cm)

A x 1   3½in (9cm)

2½in (6.5cm)

B x 2   1¾in (4.5cm)

1¾in (4.5cm)

C x 2   2¾in (7cm)

2½in (6.5cm)

D x 1   ½in (1.2cm)

1⁄16in (1.5mm) basswood sheet

2½in (6.5cm)

E x 2

2⅜in (6.3cm)

⅛in (3mm) square wooden dowel

2½in (6.5cm)

F x 1

2¼in (5.7cm)

G x 3

1½in (4cm)

H x 7

⅛in (3mm) basswood sheet

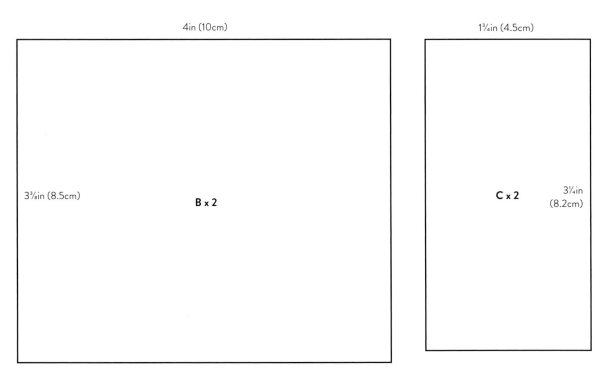

7in (17.8cm)

4in
(10cm)

A x 1

4in (10cm)

1¾in (4.5cm)

3⅜in (8.5cm)

B x 2

C x 2

3¼in
(8.2cm)

6¾in (17cm)

D x 2

3⅜in
(8.5cm)

6¾in (17cm)

E x 1

1¾in
(4.5cm)

3⅜in (8.5cm)

F x 2

2in
(⁵cm)

2½in (6.5cm)

G x 3

2in (⁵cm)

Bathroom

⅛in (3mm) basswood sheet

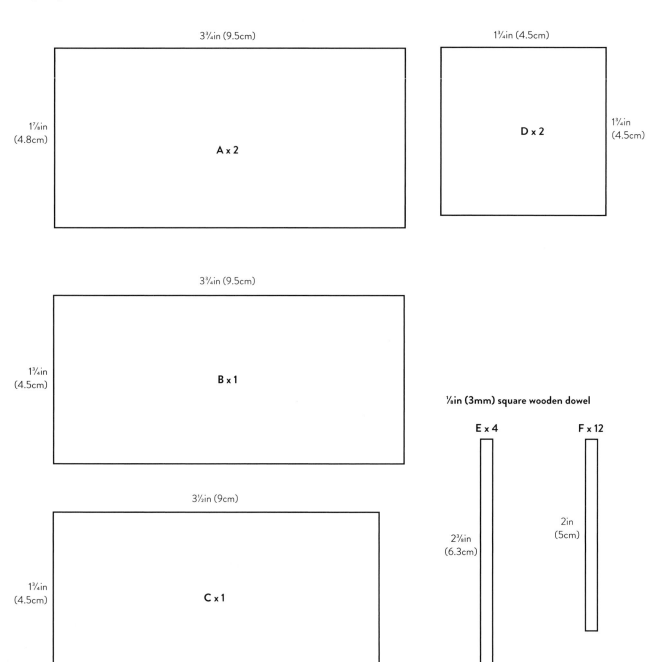

3¾in (9.5cm)

1⅞in
(4.8cm)

A x 2

1¾in (4.5cm)

D x 2

1¾in
(4.5cm)

3¾in (9.5cm)

1¾in
(4.5cm)

B x 1

⅛in (3mm) square wooden dowel

3½in (9cm)

1¾in
(4.5cm)

C x 1

E x 4

F x 12

2⅜in
(6.3cm)

2in
(5cm)

BATHTUB

¼in (6mm) foamcore

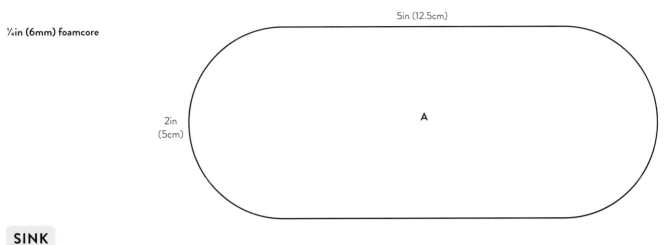

5in (12.5cm)

2in
(5cm)

A

SINK

¼in (6mm) foamcore

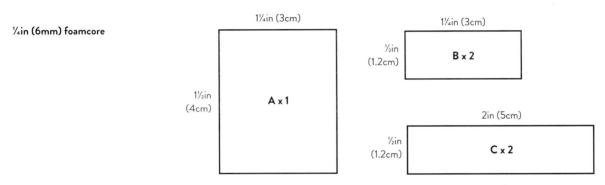

1¼in (3cm)

A x 1

1½in
(4cm)

1¼in (3cm)

½in
(1.2cm)

B x 2

2in (5cm)

½in
(1.2cm)

C x 2

TOILET

¼in (6mm) foamcore

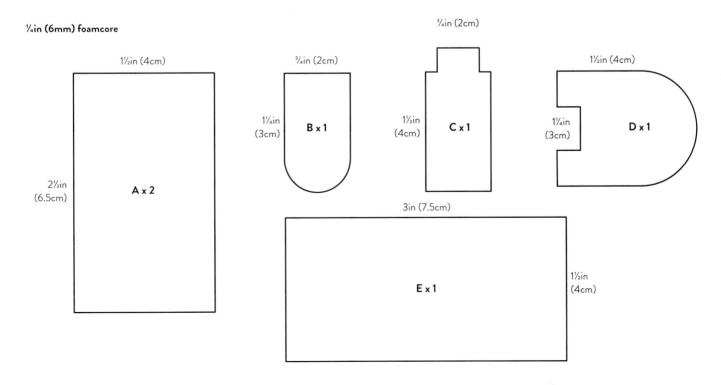

1½in (4cm)

A x 2

2½in
(6.5cm)

¾in (2cm)

1¼in
(3cm)

B x 1

¾in (2cm)

1½in
(4cm)

C x 1

1½in (4cm)

1¼in
(3cm)

D x 1

3in (7.5cm)

E x 1

1½in
(4cm)

Bedroom

⅛in (3mm) basswood sheet

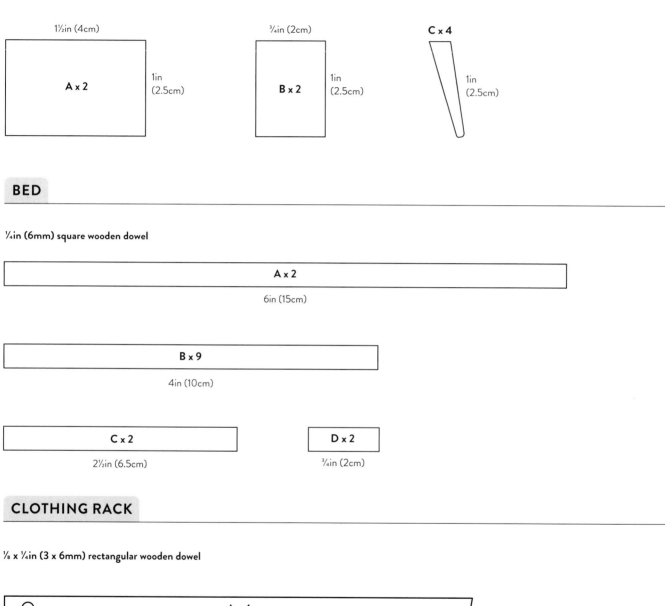

1½in (4cm)

A x 2

1in (2.5cm)

¾in (2cm)

B x 2

1in (2.5cm)

C x 4

1in (2.5cm)

BED

¼in (6mm) square wooden dowel

A x 2

6in (15cm)

B x 9

4in (10cm)

C x 2

2½in (6.5cm)

D x 2

¾in (2cm)

CLOTHING RACK

⅛ x ¼in (3 x 6mm) rectangular wooden dowel

A x 4

5in (12.5cm)

B x 1

2¾in (7cm)

C x 1

3in (7.5cm)

Patio

¼in (6mm) square wooden dowel

A x 2

6½in (16.5cm)

B x 2

2¼in (5.7cm)

F x 4

¾in (2cm)

⅛ x ¼in (3 x 6mm) rectangular wooden dowel

C x 2

2in (5cm)

D x 2

2¼in (5.7cm)

E x 2

2¾in (7cm)

SLING CHAIR

¼in (6mm) square wooden dowel

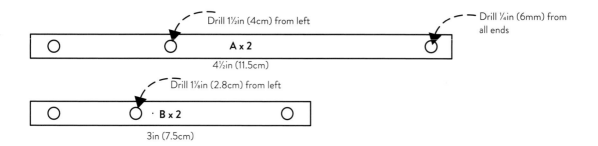

Drill 1½in (4cm) from left

Drill ¼in (6mm) from all ends

A x 2

4½in (11.5cm)

Drill 1⅛in (2.8cm) from left

B x 2

3in (7.5cm)

⅛in (3mm) square wooden dowel

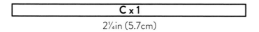

C x 1

2¼in (5.7cm)

PALM PLANT

Paper

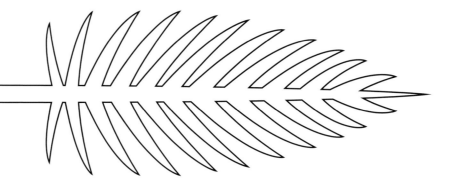

Photo: Michelle Gevint

ABOUT THE AUTHOR

Chelsea Andersson is the maker and miniaturist behind ChelseaMakes. Her miniatures are used in television, stop-motion advertisements, and of course, to decorate dollhouses.

Having started her professional career as a landscape architect, Chelsea enjoys design and understanding how objects and spaces are built. Outside of the office, she spent her time creating miniatures: tiny versions of a dream home she hoped to one day build. She crafted hundreds of tiny objects for herself, and for her hamster Martin, before deciding to share this love of making with other creators. She went on to design and manufacture a line of Do-It-Yourself dollhouses called Simplekits.

Following an appearance on the crafting competition TV show *Making It*, Chelsea was finally confident enough to pursue her love of making, and miniatures, full time.

Today she lives in Connecticut with her husband Nick and cat Millie. Together they are working to renovate their dream home at full size. When not in her craft studio, Chelsea can be found hiking in the forest or working on home renovation projects.

SUPPLIERS

One of my favorite things about making miniatures is how accessible it is. Even without fancy tools and materials, you can create hundreds of incredible tiny objects. After all, your project only requires a little bit of any one material. Look around your home, at your existing craft tools, in your scrap piles and rubbish bins, and see what can be made from what you already have.

For additional materials and tools mentioned in this book, visit your local art, hobby, or craft stores.

For additional miniatures, and easy-to-assemble kits, explore chelseamakes.com

ACKNOWLEDGMENTS

To my husband Nick: Thank you for turning the lights on when I work late into the night. You make life more fun, more exciting, and so much easier. I love you.

To my family and friends: Even when my ideas seemed silly, or strange, you championed them all. You are the loudest, most enthusiastic cheering section I could ever hope for. Thank you for creating with me.

To Coco Peri: You gave me permission to pursue a creative, happy, playful life. Thank you for opening the door.

To the David and Charles team: Thank you for helping me bring this book to life. I never would have dreamed that this was something I was capable of. I am so proud of what we have created together.

Index

A DAVID AND CHARLES BOOK
© David and Charles, Ltd 2023

David and Charles is an imprint of David and Charles, Ltd
Suite A, Tourism House, Pynes Hill, Exeter, EX2 5WS

Text and Designs © Chelsea Andersson 2023
Layout and Photography © David and Charles, Ltd 2023

First published in the UK and USA in 2023

A catalogue record for this book is available from the British Library.

ISBN-13: 9781446309940 paperback
ISBN-13: 9781446309957 EPUB
ISBN-13: 9781446310311 PDF

This book has been printed on paper from approved suppliers and made from pulp from sustainable sources.

Printed in China through Asia Pacific Offset for:
David and Charles, Ltd
Suite A, Tourism House, Pynes Hill, Exeter, EX2 5WS

10 9 8 7 6 5 4 3 2 1

Publishing Director: Ame Verso
Senior Commissioning Editor: Sarah Callard
Managing Editor: Jeni Chown
Editor: Jessica Cropper
Project Editor: Sarah Hoggett
Head of Design: Anna Wade
Design and Art Direction: Prudence Rogers
Illustrations: Chelsea Andersson
Pre-press Designer: Ali Stark
Photography: Jason Jenkins and Chelsea Andersson
Production Manager: Beverley Richardson

David and Charles publishes high-quality books on a wide range of subjects. For more information visit
www.davidandcharles.com.

Share your makes with us on social media using #dandcbooks and follow us on Facebook and Instagram by
searching for @dandcbooks.

Layout of the digital edition of this book may vary depending on reader hardware and display settings.